The POLICY
P ~ P
P R E S S

COMMUNITY
DEVELOPMENT
FOUNDATION

First published in Great Britain in 1999 by
The Policy Press
34 Tyndall's Park Road
Bristol BS8 1PY
UK

Tel no +44 (0)117 954 6800
Fax no +44 (0)117 973 7308
E-mail tpp@bristol.ac.uk
http://www.bristol.ac.uk/Publications/TPP

ISBN 1 86134 188 1

Claire Freeman is Senior Lecturer (Planning), Otago University, New Zealand,
Paul Henderson is Director, Practice Development, Community Development
Foundation and **Jane Kettle** is Senior Lecturer (Planning and Housing), Leeds
Metropolitan University.

The photographs in this publication are © The Children's Society and modelled
for The Children's Society, unless otherwise stated.

Cover design by Qube Design Associates, Bristol.
Photograph kindly supplied by www.johnbirdsall.co.uk
Printed in Great Britain by Hobbs the Printers Ltd, Southampton

Contents

Preface

Preparation of this book has been informed by a wide range of local projects, in particular by examples known to us in the city of Leeds and by case studies of children's participation undertaken by consultants in other parts of the country. We make considerable use of both sources throughout the book.

The sources have helped to reinforce some points and to throw new light on others. Above all, however, they have provided a channel for children's voices to be part of the book. The following statements are taken from children's charters which were drawn up by groups in two of the case study areas. They touch on many of the issues and themes addressed in the book:

> Adults' and children's needs are basically the same but it is how they are treated in obtaining what they need that is the difference. There is a communication problem because children aren't treated as seriously as an adult would be in the same situation. This is why there is such a strong borderline between the decision-makers and the young whom the decision will concern. (Bedford Children's Charter)

> We feel that children are not aware of what is going on regarding planning and building, especially houses on the green belt as this takes away our playing fields and our rural environment. Once we have found out about plans they have already been completed and further consultation is not taken into account. For example, on a local playing field a popular climbing frame was changed for an ugly plastic replacement. This is much more easily vandalised and is not as popular with children. We feel that for such a project, consultation of local children should take place, the involved age range should have a say in this type of project, eg there could be a competition in a school/library. (Rochdale Children's Charter)

Acknowledgements

We would like to acknowledge the influence of the workshop presenters on examples of children's participation at a national conference held in Manchester in 1996. It was the extent and variety of the examples that motivated us to write this book. Similarly, a large number of practitioners – too many to list – have provided further examples. Quite literally, we could not have written the book without their help.

Our decision to ask three consultants to work with groups of children and young people to develop material for the book was a natural extension of the conference experience. We are grateful to Margaret Lindsay, Chris Smith and Wayne Talbot for the care they took in planning, running and writing up the consultations, and to the children and young people who agreed to take part in the consultations and gave up their time to do so. Our thanks go also to our families who have been enormously patient and supportive throughout the process of discussing and writing the book.

The project benefited from receiving a grant from the Calouste Gulbenkian Foundation. We appreciate this support as well as the encouragement given by the Foundation's Deputy Director, Paul Curno. We are grateful also to Dawn Louise Pudney of The Policy Press for the support she has given.

ONE

Setting the scene

The right of children to participate more fully in societies of which they form a part received increasing recognition during the 1990s. Much of the impetus stemmed from the United Nations (UN) Convention on the Rights of the Child (1989) and from the UN Conference on Environment and Development (1992). But not all of it.

Equally significant were the actions of children themselves, many of them small-scale and many of them undertaken with adults. These actions did not represent a groundswell, and often the participants met barriers and scepticism, but across the world a pattern can be observed. It is with the intention of getting inside this development that this book has been written. We refer throughout to the 'big picture' – the policies and legislation of governments, the global as well as the local – but the focus is on action and activities in the United Kingdom generated by and on behalf of children. The extent and range of these is astonishing:

- City-wide initiatives being taken by children's organisations to build coalitions of those working with children and young people to support children's participation.
- Neighbourhood resources – schools, youth clubs, family centres – which provide vital support for children and young people.
- Action taken by children and young people themselves either through formally constituted bodies, such as forums and youth councils, or through informal groups and networks.

We intersperse details of these and other projects within the text. We also draw upon specially commissioned research undertaken with groups of children and young people in three areas: Wardle in Rochdale, Bedford, and Dunbarton in Scotland. Locally-based consultants met regularly with the groups and worked with them on a number of questions which had been agreed between them and the authors. This proved to be an invaluable way of rooting the book in the ideas and experiences of children themselves.

The book is concerned with ensuring that children's rights and participation become part of the good practice of professionals whose decisions and interventions impact so much on children's lives. We make the case for taking seriously the need to work *with* children in the processes of planning better communities. In this introductory chapter we seek to answer key questions concerning the book's topic:

- What are 'better communities'?
- How are we using the term 'children'?
- Who is involved in working for children?
- Where has the issue of children's participation come from?

We go on to discuss the book's purpose and why we have chosen to give it a UK focus rather than a global one. In a concluding section of this chapter we summarise the key questions to be explored, identify some underlying dilemmas and explain the structure of the book.

'Better communities'

A sea-change has taken place in how policy makers talk about 'community'. Definitional contortions on the meaning of community have been left behind because of awareness of the urgent need to address the problems facing poor, alienated communities. The change can be seen most clearly in the Social Exclusion Unit's report *Bringing Britain together: A national strategy for neighbourhood renewal* (1998). In addition to summarising research on the extent of poverty, the report focuses on the new geography of poverty, the limitations of earlier regeneration programmes and the importance of community involvement: "Success", writes the Prime Minister in the report's foreword, "depends on communities themselves having the power and taking the responsibility to make things better" (Social Exclusion Unit, 1998). The same message is given in the plans for the government's regeneration programmes, notably, the *New Deal for Communities* (DETR, 1998).

Working for better communities has become a political imperative. The argument in this book is that children need to be included in the processes and programmes of community involvement. Crucial to the latter are the criteria used to judge success or otherwise. Fortunately, there now exists a body of knowledge which enables this to be done. The following is taken from a publication which spells out how community development can be measured. We make use of two key concepts – community empowerment and quality of community life – to pinpoint the outputs and outcomes of community development:

The building blocks of community development

Community empowerment
1.   A learning community: personal empowerment
2.   A fair and just community: positive action
3.   An active and organised community: development of the community
4.   An influential community: participation and involvement

Quality of community life
5.   A commonwealth: local economic development
6.   A caring community: social development and services
7.   A green community: environmental development
8.   A safe community
9.   A good place to live
10. A lasting community

(Barr et al, 1996, p 10)

Thus the term 'better communities' can be used with confidence. There is something to aim for. It is misleading to think that the term is trapped in vagueness.

Children and young people

A few years ago one of us received a note from a manager in one of the large children's organisations, alerting us to the problem of using the term 'children':

> "We find that children is not a term which most over tens would wish to be applied to them. Although it is unwieldy we acknowledge the need to use 'children and young people' in order not to exclude either older or younger groups. Also use of either children or young people will tend to define the age group for the professional audience as well, which is a loss."

The points are taken. We believe, however, that there are two reasons why it is sometimes important to use the term 'children' on its own.

Firstly, it helps to distance the issues of rights and participation from an exclusive focus on youth work, reminding us that 5- to 11-year-olds is an age group in its own right. This point is especially important for the topic we are looking at because of its non-institutional focus –

neighbourhoods, informal groups and networks rather than more formally organised activities such as those to be found in youth clubs.

Secondly, using children as an identifiable category is consistent with research and policy outside the UK, thereby making comparisons easier. The UN Convention on the Rights of the Child (1989), for example, defines children as those under 18 years old. While this can be challenged (how many 17-year-olds call themselves children?), the fact is that it exists in the international context.

Our preference is to argue for a flexible definition of the term children because so much depends on context: social class, ethnicity, gender, geography. There is a case for distinguishing between children and young people while recognising that they fit on a continuum on which individuals (often of the same age) place themselves at different points. Being over-concerned by age may, accordingly, be misleading. This point has been made about the term young people:

> Perhaps youth is better described as the space, rather than the years, between childhood and adulthood, between childish innocence and the full independence which arrives with an earned income, more permanent relationships and perhaps an independent home of one's own.... Thinking in terms of 'transitions', from infancy to childhood, then to adolescence and on to adulthood may be more illuminating. (Wadhams, 1998, p 7)

Working for children

The ambiguity of the phrase 'working for children' is deliberate: we are concerned to examine the role of the practitioner, how they carry out work which relates to children – attitudes, methods, skills, techniques – and it is important to disentangle at least three different approaches contained in the phrase 'working for children':

- The minimalist approach where an adult or organisation simply acknowledges the need to take children's interests into account in the planning process.
- Adults and organisations committed to working *on behalf of* children. Most national children's organisations come into this category, as do the children's services plans of local authorities.

- Those who work *with children*, supporting them in their actions. Most practitioners employed by children's organisations would see themselves working in this way.

The value of the minimalist approach is questionable, but the other two, while often contrasting, are equally valid. Both need to be informed by the same participatory principles as well as by what is known about how to work for children in community settings. This knowledge base, as we shall see, is considerable.

Working for children is relevant to a broad swathe of professions and a creative feature of the topic is its interdisciplinary nature. If we look at the professions, we can see from the following categorisation the extent of the range of potential interest:

Service delivery
Planners
Housing officers
Social workers
Health staff
Programme staff
Regeneration officers
Partnership staff
Grass-roots practitioners
Community workers
Youth workers
Play workers
Drug prevention staff
Arts workers

Throughout the book we deliberately use examples and ideas from across this range. We also draw upon relevant research.

Children's participation

The issue of children's participation has developed from a number of different arenas and this goes some way towards explaining the attention it continues to receive. We provide information on the strands of development at different points in the book. Here we summarise them:

- The participation Articles of the UN Convention on the Rights of the Child (1989) and the ways in which, in the UK context, children's

rights organisations have campaigned and lobbied for its implementation.
- Opportunities provided by the 1989 Children Act.
- Academic research and theory on children's participation.
- Children's projects run by Save the Children, The Children's Society, Barnardo's and NCH Action for Children.
- The commitment of some local authorities to children's participation in the context of children's rights.
- Children's involvement in environmental action, especially in relation to Local Agenda 21.

Case study: Durham County Council has launched an 'Investment in Children' initiative. It brings together all of the organisations within the county which are important to the lives of children and young people. The statement of intent commits the organisations to consult with children, young people and their families about decisions affecting their lives and the development of services. A Children and Young People's Council has been created and it can feed views from the council to the authority's Policy and Resources Committee and other groups. Two funding sources for community groups and young people have been set up and a monthly newsletter started. It is planned to turn Investing in Children into a membership organisation. Investing in Children is part of a wider agenda which in turn is informed by government policies on social inclusion, partnership, health improvement, community safety, environmental sustainability and lifelong learning.

There is both breadth and depth behind the idea of children's participation. However, there is still some way to go. Two questions in particular need to be addressed:
- What types of participation are being used up and down the country? The reason why the ladder of participation showing different levels and types of participation (Arnstein, 1969) keeps reappearing in publications and on training courses is because there is still a lot of confusion surrounding the issue of participation. And in communities which have been consulted and invited to participate by outside agencies many times over the years, there can often be found anger and scepticism. This is because many participation schemes have been experienced as tokenistic and, perhaps even less forgivable, they have not been followed through with action. There is a need, therefore,

for some basic ground rules to be agreed on how meaningful and effective participation can be achieved.

- How can the issue of children's participation become part of mainstream policies and activities of organisations, as opposed to being perceived always in terms of 'projects'? This is often an inherent problem for many social policies in the UK: moving good practice from the margins to the mainstream. It presents both practitioners and managers with a major challenge of achieving organisational change. The issue of children's participation is undoubtedly an example of this problem.

These two unresolved questions lead us to laying out the purpose of this book. We are concerned to draw attention to key principles and examples of good practice of children's participation, and we want to show how professional practitioners can engage seriously with the issue as part of their day-to-day work; the book is designed to be a resource for them. Informing both of these objectives is a dissemination argument.

There is, firstly, a need to bring together and analyse existing knowledge and information which is directly relevant to planning with children for better communities. The amount of material available on both children's rights and children's needs is considerable and we refer to much of it throughout the text. There is, in addition, both a practice and research literature which is directly relevant to children's participation. Again, we make use of both categories at appropriate points in the book, striving to achieve a balance between, on the one hand, recognising and using existing knowledge and, on the other, allowing the writing to remain accessible.

Secondly, writing this book represents a significant milestone in the work we have done in recent years on children and communities:

- Research and consultancy on children's involvement in Local Agenda 21 issues in Manchester and Leeds. The Manchester work was undertaken for the local authority; the Leeds work was a special project carried out with the local authority.
- Research on children's involvement in regeneration schemes.
- A national conference, held in Manchester in 1996, which brought together practitioners interested and involved in working for children. The inputs and workshops at the event were inspiring and it was these which led directly to the decision to produce the book.
- The publication of four briefing papers (CDF, 1998) which summarise and update the material in the book *Children and communities* (Henderson, 1995). The papers were disseminated through national

children's and community development organisations. This experience reinforced our wish to contribute further to the dissemination of key ideas and practice examples.

• Finally, we were fortunate to obtain funding from the Gulbenkian Foundation to enable us to employ three consultants to work with groups of children and young people in different parts of the country directly on the book's themes.

We make use of the findings and outcomes of all of the above pieces of work, integrating them with the developments in this country and elsewhere referred to earlier.

The combination of wishing to draw together existing material and our own experiences enabled us to specify the following aims for the book:

• to present the case for children's participation in planning and decision making;
• to show the importance of the neighbourhood for children, especially for their rights to play and for safety;
• to provide examples of children's participation in neighbourhoods;
• to set out the implications for professionals when supporting children's participation;
• to make the case for children's involvement in urban and rural regeneration;
• to set out a future agenda for supporting children's participation.

UK focus

Our instinct when first planning the book was to place it in the global context, because of the universality of the issue of children's participation and the international significance of the UN Convention on the Rights of the Child and the 1992 Rio conference. Further reflection moved us away from using this framework, chiefly because of our concern to address directly the roles and responsibilities of practitioners and managers whose work has the potential to involve children. Grounding the ideas and examples within the organisational and training structures of the UK made this more feasible than using a global framework would have done. We want the material in the book not only to be read but also to be applied. Using the UK context as the main but not exclusive focus makes this more likely because we can stay close to the realities of local communities and to the pressures and opportunities experienced by local professionals. Adopting this approach does not, of course, reduce in any way the significance of the global.

Key questions ... and dilemmas

Readers will find that, in all the chapters, we return to some fundamental questions concerning children's participation. They are, in our opinion, questions to which there are no obvious answers yet which cannot be sidestepped. We summarise them at this point as follows:

- What are the key issues – local, national and global – *as far as children themselves are concerned?* What are their likes and dislikes, and how do they want to be consulted about these issues and become involved with them?
- How can the agendas of *children's rights* organisations, operating within the framework of the UN Convention on the Rights of the Child, be better integrated with community development work being undertaken in response to *children's needs?*
- In what ways do children *perceive and value neighbourhoods?* Is the neighbourhood meaningful to children and, if so, how can they become more involved with it?
- In *regeneration programmes, what are the 'trigger points' for involving children?* Is it possible to identify practice principles which are common to regeneration programmes?
- How can *professional practitioners* work most effectively with and on behalf of children? To achieve this, what are the key learning points between professions such as planning, social work, youth work, play work and regeneration?

These are testing questions and it is important to avoid suggesting that there are simple answers to them. Indeed, the issue of children's participation raises several major dilemmas.

Children and adults

The new sociology of childhood places considerable emphasis on childhood as a social phenomenon: "in this new approach the focus is on *childhood* as a social construction resulting from the collective actions of *children* with adults and each other." (Corsaro, 1997, p 43). Any discussion of children's participation has, as a result, to engage with adult, society-wide ideas and policies; it cannot be restricted only to a children's framework. A simple example is the evidence of the extent to which children's time outside school has increasingly become regulated by adults – a wide range of organised activities for children, being taken to school by car and so on. Such decisions, whether negotiated or not, involve adults as well as children. Given this context, the dilemma facing advocates of children's participation is knowing how much effort to put into working with children, how much with adults and how much with them jointly. There are so many variables that, in the worst case scenario, advocates and children themselves could easily become immobilised by uncertainty. At the very least, they usually have to analyse a range of factors and consider a number of options. Planning with children for better communities offers no quick or easy answers.

Competing priorities

Those organisations which are committed to children's participation will tend to have high expectations of what can be achieved: they are keen to see results and achievements. Yet are the expectations sometimes too high? We ask the question in relation to two issues. Firstly, there are enormous pressures on all children – within the education system, from the media and popular culture, from commercial organisations – to behave and act in certain ways. Some of these are in tension with the ideas behind children's participation; others can be seen more as competitors for children's time, attention and spending power. Whatever one thinks of these pressures, the fact is that they exist. It is within this social and cultural context that the agenda for children's participation has to operate. Perhaps we should not be surprised if sometimes it is pushed down the list of priorities?

Secondly, research findings on children and poverty point to factors which work against children's participation. Unstable family situations, high crime rates, the effects of high adult unemployment rates and low income can mean that the issue of participation becomes of secondary importance. Too many other imperatives are impacting upon the lives of children and their families. The concept of social exclusion means precisely what it says: excluded from participating in normal processes of participation. Because child poverty can limit the scope for children's participation, the two issues have to be worked on together: the government's commitment to eradicating child poverty in 20 years needs to include measures which will help children to be full members of society.

The existence of very powerful consumer pressures and the realities of poverty are positioned, in a sense, in opposition to children's participation. Together they present a genuine dilemma for those people and organisations involved in supporting children's participation because they signal that there are issues other than participation which are important for children.

Children's safety

That society has become much more alert to the issue of children's safety is an understatement. In all kinds of contexts – schools, clubs, and public transport – there is both an acute awareness of the issue and regulations or procedures aimed at protecting children. The concern with children's well-being, including while they are playing in their own neighbourhoods, is understandable. The extent of violent crimes against children, and better reporting of child abuse, has resulted in an increased understanding of the problem. It is essential for those organisations involved with children's participation to recognise the degree of public anxiety concerning children's safety. Inevitably it will place constraints on how, when and where activities are organised. The case for participation will get nowhere if these questions are not addressed. This can be said to be a dilemma in the sense that planning children's involvement has to be part of other agendas.

Long term and short term

Participation needs to be a long-term activity. Schemes which last only a few weeks and which do not reappear bring about little change. Indeed they can be counterproductive because they can lead to cynicism. And yet opportunities for supporting children's participation are often short term. This is partly to do with the 'project' culture in UK social policy referred to earlier – funding a small number of schemes for two or three years – and partly a recognition of the public's willingness to donate funds to children's projects from which there will be immediate tangible results – new play equipment, a holiday scheme and so on. The processes required to plan, set up, run and evaluate participation schemes usually lack this immediacy.

In putting forward the above four dilemmas, we are not wanting to diminish the potential offered by children's participation. Rather we are urging those who are involved, or who plan to become involved, to avoid framing the issue too narrowly or too idealistically. We believe it is timely to make this point strongly. Children's participation has a very good track record over the last 10 years: campaigns and projects have mushroomed and there have been some excellent results. Now, however, the experience needs to be transferred into the mainstream of planning and service delivery organisations and for this to happen, the wider societal context of children in the UK at the end of the 20th century must receive greater recognition.

The book's structure

The significance of the last point is reflected in the sequencing of the book's chapters. Chapter 2 provides an overview of the position of children in the UK today, Chapter 3 discusses the UN Convention on the Rights of the Child in the context of children's needs and current legislation on children, and Chapter 4 places the issue of children's participation in the political context, especially the government's commitment to social inclusion. In Chapter 5 we set out the ways in which community development can support children's involvement, concentrating on grass-roots work but looking too at the need for work to be done at the level of policy in local authorities, health and government agencies. In Chapters 6 and 7 we examine the roles of other professionals in being able to work for children and the particular opportunities offered by regeneration programmes. Chapter 8 contains material on the options available for shaping the social and physical environments of children and in Chapter 9 we take this one step further by specifying the conditions needed to support children's participation: how their involvement can become an integral part of professional practice and relate to the issues of social inclusion and sustainability.

TWO

The contemporary context

© www.johnbirdsall.co.uk

Diverse and confusing worlds

Children in the UK in the 1990s experienced a confused and confusing world. They found themselves bombarded with advice: salads are healthier than chips, avoid unsafe sex. Images proliferated: billboards targeted at children, adverts for ChildLine (the children's crisis phoneline), megastores, exotic holidays. Other images and experiences are more subtle and less unambiguously negative: signs on shops saying 'no unaccompanied children', 'no ball games' on housing estates, and the removal of seating from shopping centres to discourage 'loitering' youth. On the positive side, children's environmental knowledge is given considerable publicity: photographs in local newspapers of children planting trees (usually together with a local dignitary), schools undertaking litter clean-ups, and playground 'greening' projects.

What do these images convey? How do children make sense of them? How do they relate to children's own life experiences?

Children inhabit a complex and contradictory society. It is full of mixed messages, not only about what it stands for but also about what it expects and offers to its young people. On the one hand, it eulogises children's environmental actions when it comes to tree planting, but condemns young people who undertake tree-top protests at Newbury and elsewhere, where trees have to give way to roads and other 'economically beneficial' developments. Given this bewildering diversity of images that society portrays, how is it possible to gain any coherent understanding of the lives of children? The answer is that it is not possible. At best an approximation of children's lives can be portrayed, reflecting common experiences, ideas, beliefs and hopes. Children's lives are as different as adults', influenced by their race, class, gender, health, location, and the attitudes, facilities and opportunities provided by their communities. This chapter explores the changing nature of children's lives, the opportunities provided and the constraints imposed. It considers the issues that are important in understanding children's lives: their families, social conditions and relations and, most importantly, the issues that children consider to be important in their lives.

Children's lives: changing social demography

Fewer children

Children's experience of society is influenced both by the kind of family into which they are born and by the nature of the wider society. Within both of these contexts children will be influenced by their experiences of how they relate to adults and the adult world. The role of children is also influenced by changing population trends. The number of under 16-year-olds in the UK declined from 14.2 million in 1971 to around 12 million in 1995 (Central Statistical Office, in Sparks, 1995). Conversely the proportion of the population aged over 65 is increasing from 11.7 million in 1961 to an expected 15.7 million in 2001, rising again to 19.4 million in 2021 (Central Statistical Office, in Sparks, 1995).

The impact of these demographic changes are viewed with some concern by many professionals and others interested in children's welfare. Sgritta, for example, hypothesises that "demographic change has helped to alter profoundly the system of rules governing the allocation of resources to diverse groups of the population" (Sgritta, 1994, p 335). Per capita spending on children in the UK, though higher than in other countries studied by Sgritta, was still only one fifth the per capita spending for elderly people. He argues that over the last 25 years, the "welfare state for youth" has been remoulded into a "welfare state for the ageing". While acknowledging that support for elderly people is a fundamental duty of society, it is essential to ensure, particularly given the superior numerical and political clout that elderly people have, that this support is not at the expense of children.

In addressing issues relating to children's social experience it is useful to start by analysing the family, as it is through the family that children first experience wider society. The family in the 1990s was subject to intense pressures and has been the focus of considerable change, change which has substantial implications for children.

Families and children

It is through the family environment that children begin their interaction with and absorption into wider society. The family is the prime determinant of the child's life chances. Families meet children's needs in three key ways:

- By providing whole and lasting relationships between child and parents.
- Through the division and organisation of the family's living space. In almost all national reports it is stated that children live in more crowded conditions than the rest of the population, a fact that presents a serious challenge to those in the housing profession. The situation can be further exacerbated by the division of space within the household, a situation in which children can be marginalised in terms of which space they can use.
- In its everyday life, the family should provide a flexible reaction to the needs of the child: "the family must therefore be made available as an environment suitable for children, and it must also open the way to extra-familial environments suitable for children" (Englebert, 1994, p 292).

In meeting these needs the family, while providing stability, has also to be flexible in its relationship with society as a whole, and adaptable in meeting children's needs.

Fewer adults with responsibility for children

Significant changes are also being observed in the distribution of children in society. Research undertaken by Coleman (in Qvortrup, 1994) found that the number of childless households increased from 27% in 1870 to

64% in 1983. It is a figure that has serious implications for children's welfare. On the plus side it means that adults who do not wish to become parents or who are not suited to parenting feel able to take a positive decision to remain childless. It does, however, mean that the responsibility for children's financial, emotional and general well-being has become the charge of a decreasing proportion of the adult population. In mitigation it could be argued that in practice, responsibility, at least in the financial sense, is spread across a wider range of the adult population through the tax contributions to healthcare, schools, maternity leave and other primarily child-oriented services. The emotional and supportive aspects of child-rearing, however, are not so widely distributed, with many parents bringing up children in conditions where little, if any, community support is received.

The situation becomes of even greater concern on closer examination of the family setting in which children grow up, where the number of adults in households is also decreasing. In 1972, 91% of children were brought up in two-parent families. By 1992 this had fallen to 79%. This is a significant increase in the number of children being brought up in one-parent families. The impact of single parenting on children's welfare and development is unclear and is a matter that is being debated with some vigour by sociologists, politicians and society as a whole. What is less debatable is the fact that children in single-parent families tend to be concentrated at the lower end of the economic spectrum where poverty is endemic. It is generally accepted that poverty has serious implications for children's educational, health and future life prospects.

Families with fewer children

An interesting parallel to the change in family size and structure has been the general decline in the number of children in each family. In his study of the historical transformation of children's lives in the USA, Hernandez (1993) found that 82% of adolescents born in 1865 lived in families with five or more children. By 1930 this figure had dropped to 30%. Saporiti (1994) also examined changing family size between 1987-92. The research had as its focus an examination of 'childhood as a social phenomenon'. The statistics on changing family sizes in Europe provided by Saporiti's research endorse the trend identified by Hernandez of smaller families. In the 1980s the percentage of children living in families with four or more children for selected countries were as follows: Denmark 1%; Italy 6%; Finland 3%; USA 5%; and West Germany 2%.

The UK figure was not included but is unlikely to be dissimilar. The impact of declining family size on children requires further analysis. Saporiti poses a number of questions that need addressing:

- What does the 'disappearance of children' imply with respect to childhood?
- Does it mean a progressive lowering in the rank of childhood status among different social priorities?
- Could it not be that the 'rarefaction' of children makes them "a more precious good", more appreciated and valued? (Saporiti, 1994, p 210)

In particular it will be necessary to assess the effect that this decline in sibling numbers has had on children's socialisation both within and outside the family. The decline in family size suggests that the provision of socialisation opportunities for children outside the family is a matter to which society needs to give careful consideration.

Not only are children affected by changing family dynamics but also by changing political, economic and other social influences. These can have direct impact on children's well-being and on their ability to articulate their societal needs. In order to meet these needs there has to be recognition of the diversity of children's needs, experiences and aspirations.

Social conditions in the 1990s

Different children, different opportunities

It sounds trite to say that all children are different, but use of the generic term children can hide huge discrepancies, the most obvious being the difference between boys and girls. The International Save the Children Alliance (ISCA) emphasises this point, stating that "gender neutral terms such as children, teenagers, adolescents and youth can perpetuate the greater invisibility of girls and adolescent women in the eyes of policymakers and funders ..." (ISCA, undated, p 3). ISCA stresses the need to ensure that the principles of the UN Convention on the Rights of the Child are in fact applied equally to both boys and girls. The Convention's four principles of non-discrimination when applied to girls "set out a clear and uncompromising commitment to a girl's right to development as an individual:

- that girls have equal value as human beings;
- that the best interests of girls should be primary;

- that due weight be given to the opinion of girls;
- that every girl has rights" (ISCA, undated).

The need for awareness of gender differences is especially important when examining children's participation in decision making and other public processes, as it is in those circumstances where the tendency is for girls to take a 'back seat'.

In analysing children's experiences and their environments it is also necessary to recognise that boys' and girls' experiences can be significantly different. A well-known example is the differing levels of freedom experienced by girls and boys and the implications this has with regard to accessing their environment. Research into children's independent mobility clearly shows that the independent mobility of boys is substantially higher than that for girls (Hillman, 1993; Tranter, 1993; Freeman, 1995). So the neighbourhood and wider environment in which children live can be more accessible to boys than girls. Children's experiences, attitudes and approaches can also be influenced by disability, in which case the physical environment can be particularly significant. Other influences include culture and ethnicity, particularly important given the increasingly diverse, multicultural nature of British society.

Critical to children's social situation is the development of a sense of belonging. It is a 'sense' that is determined both by reference to the immediate family and immediate social networks and also to mainstream assumptions and attitudes to a child's ethnic, language, religious and other affiliations. These mainstream assumptions can be significant factors in determining not only cultural but also environmental attitudes and experiences. An obvious example is that children who feel unsafe due to racial harassment may feel disinclined to range beyond the immediate vicinity of their home, thus being cut off from access to environmental benefits located further afield, such as parks and sports grounds. Even at a very young age, children are able to respond to racial issues in ways that imply quite complex levels of social awareness. One of the difficulties that Connolly (1995) identifies as being experienced by those researching children and race, and one that will confront professionals working in this arena, is that racism is not a given but is a 'process' whereby "the salience, meaning and effects of 'race' will vary from one context to the next ... [racism] can only be understood through the dynamics of social activity" (Connolly, 1995, p 176).

Professionals, therefore, will need to be alert to the fact that children are not a static homogeneous group. Their differences and the evolving and changing nature of their life experiences must be recognised. In doing so it will be necessary to acknowledge both the positive and negative influences associated with 'difference'. For example, culture can significantly influence children's ability to engage with their local environment. Its influence can be especially important, and in some cases especially restrictive, for girls. Conversely it is necessary to appreciate the richness that comes with diversity, through different religions, cultures, ethnic groups, languages, geographical location and so on. These contribute to the life experiences that children bring to the participative process and consequently influence their attitudes and understanding of their environment. In any assessment, it is necessary to recognise that children can experience a multiplicity of influences which may act to further enhance or reduce their interactions with society and their environment.

Children and the economy

Perhaps the area of greatest change in the lives of children in the UK over the last 100 years has been their removal from being active participants in the economy to being economic dependants. The question of children's participation in the economy is a difficult one, characterised by the primary need to protect children from exploitation. In response to the question of 'what is the place of children in civil society?', Gabarino states that the child "is to be shielded from the *direct* demands of economic, political and sexual forces. Children have a claim on their parents, and they have a right to receive support from their families and their communities, regardless of their economic value in accounting terms" (Gabarino, in Kent, 1995, p 5). Although children's role in the economy has undoubtedly decreased, many children still participate in the economy.

It is difficult to be certain about the number of child workers as underage workers are normally excluded from national labour statistics. It is estimated that official figures for child labour reflect only about 10% of the real figure (Boyden with Holden, 1991, p 118). Boyden's concern was primarily with children in the South, but it is likely that similar under-reporting of child labour rates exists in the North. It has been estimated that 40% of 11- to 16-year-olds in the UK undertake some form of labour (Morrow, 1994). Many children work outside the formal sector and, as such, share the experiences of those in the informal sector: lack of safety checks, uncontrolled working hours and no minimum pay rates.

Children can have a role in the economy in their own right but they are particularly vulnerable to the impact of economic processes on the family and society. Market mechanisms and doctrines, economic recession, restructuring, spending decisions, unemployment and other facets of the economy directly influence children's opportunities. When decisions are taken with regard to economic change it is essential that both the direct and indirect impacts of this change on children are considered. Article 32 of the UN Convention specifies children's right to be protected from economic exploitation. However, research in the UK indicates that rates of pay for children who work are low and the risks to their health and safety high (Lavalette, 1994; Pettitt, 1998).

Health and the environment

Environment is becoming a matter of growing concern for children and especially for young people. In addition to having access to healthy living environments children and young people need access to information on health matters such as drugs, substance abuse and AIDS, which are matters of grave concern for both groups. Yet the environment as such can have a critical influence on children's health – and children themselves are becoming increasingly aware of this. A research project in Leeds, for example, looked at ways in which children and young people could participate in planning. It found that environmental issues ranked high among their concerns – alongside crime, safety and vandalism (Ruse, 1997).

There are several reasons why children are more affected by the environment than adults. In his study for the National Children's Bureau, Rosenbaum (1993) identified a number of the reasons and we have adapted these as follows:

Physiology

- Their small size means that a particle of pollution will have a bigger effect.

- In relation to their size they inhale more air and drink more water than adults. They have a proportionately greater surface area than adults and thus are more susceptible to chemicals absorbed through the skin.

- Their airways are narrower, making them more susceptible to air-born pollutants affecting respiration.

- Their immune systems are less developed, particularly for gastric diseases.

- Toxins can seriously impair children's development in the long term, eg lead pollution has been associated with brain damage.

Behaviour

- Children tend to spend longer outdoors so are more exposed to pollution, including car fumes, and dust containing lead. Their size can exacerbate the problem – as with smaller children being closer to car exhausts.

- They play in dangerous environments, eg derelict industrial sites.

- They have greater contact with the ground which can be contaminated, eg dog mess.

- Young people are more particularly vulnerable to crime, threatening behaviour and sexual offences, crimes which have a high level of under-reporting. (Sparks, 1995, p 11)

Status

- Poorer children from social groups with least influence can face the greatest problems through poor housing, and poor outdoor environments.

- Buildings and the built environment are designed to cater for adults, eg heavy doors which spring back and can injure children, handrails on stairs at adult height.

- Children have no say in the allocation of health policy and resources.

- They are exposed to effects of negative health practices indulged in by adults, eg smoking.

Clearly, children's health improved substantially in the 20th century, but, as the above list shows, there is no room for complacency. Children's environments can be unhealthy, especially for those children in low socio-economic groups. The idea of sustainable development is dominant within government policy making, and the relationship between a sustainable environment and health is recognised – in principle at least. The Inquiry into Inequalities in Health specifies that the health of families with children should be given high priority, and discusses the role of housing and the environment in determining health (Acheson, 1998). What is needed now is to acknowledge the links through action.

Children and politics

Children's futures are largely determined by governments. It is governments that distribute resources deciding, for example, on whether to spend on education or the military. It is understandable that the re-election imperative, which necessitates the maintenance of the adult electorate, is a major concern for governments, but they also need to concern themselves with children's needs and rights, ensuring that these are addressed in all government policy decisions.

Even where there is a will on the part of governments and decision makers to listen and involve, the end result can fall far short of that which was envisaged. A clear example of this occurred at the UN Conference on Environment and Development in Rio in 1992. At the Youth Forum, which paralleled the main Forum, 300 young people from 97 countries gathered to produce a youth statement covering issues from poverty to pollution. Their experience was as follows:

> Official youth were promised an hour ... when they arrived, they were told they had only ten minutes. Two minutes in the TV cameras were turned off; reporters in the press room couldn't hear. When the youth tried to tell the eager press what they'd said, UN police arrested them for holding an 'illegal press conference'.... Children were also snubbed. A group called Voice of the Children had organised hearings around the world. It was the Prime Minister of Norway's idea and she promised to bring six world leaders to hear their statement. None came. She didn't turn up herself.... (Peace Child International, 1994, p 80)

The problems experienced by youth at Rio are not confined to the world stage but pervade society generally. Save the Children echoes the views of many children's organisations:

> In the debate over children's lives one set of voices is absent: that of children and young people themselves. Their experiences of modern life are little known, their views are rarely sought or publicised and they are generally not encouraged to participate in the organisation and development of community activity in partnership with adults.

> But children and young people do have contributions to make. They have expert knowledge of the behaviour of children and young people, and what this implies – at school, on the streets, in youth clubs, in the leisure centre, in the family and so on. They also have views on what could be done to improve the environment, make the streets safe and make schools better places to study and learn. What is more, when children are offered an opportunity to assume responsibility for themselves and for others, they repeatedly demonstrate how able and willing they are to take it. (Save the Children, 1997, p 5)

Children have knowledge and understanding of their lives and the communities in which they live that needs to be acknowledged and expressed. Governments and elected politicians seek to work on behalf of everyone, a goal which is particularly important when it is often difficult for people to speak for themselves, as is the case with children. One proposal that is gaining momentum and which is supported by a number of organisations is lowering the voting age to 16. Save the Children has this as one of its major policy targets. For younger children, direct voting representation is not a possibility. If governments are to take into account the needs, views and aspirations of children it is incumbent upon them to ensure that they are informed through the representations of children themselves.

Social relations: children and adults

Power and alienation

Adults define the actions which are considered to be important or not. Important actions are thus invariably associated with adult rather than child-centred behaviour. Adult centredness continually evidences itself in even simple adult concepts of children's actions, for example, where adults discuss, children chatter; where adults learn, experiment and acquire knowledge, children play. Thus activities can be accorded profoundly different levels of significance simply through the terminology used. Adults' negative perceptions of the importance of and rationale for children's activities have been a key determinant of children's exclusion from many aspects of society. Children participate in a society where power relations are extremely unequal:

> The relationship between adults and children is therefore most likely not regulated philosophically, but by power and interests. If children are treated differently from adults the reason is not that they are not active but that they are not active in the way in which adults are active. (Qvortrup, 1994, p 4)

Where society is structured so as to ensure that adults hold all the power, it is understandable that children will experience feelings of alienation in relation to that society. There are two sides to children's alienation: the alienation that children feel in their relationship with society, and the alienation that results from negative attitudes by society towards children and young people. In their analysis of youth in contemporary society, Roche and Tucker describe children's feelings of alienation from society as follows:

> Many young people, in different social locations, feel as if they do not belong and as if they do not count; there is a growing sense of despair, of having been abandoned ... whether they are trapped without jobs on run-down inner city housing estates, are on the receiving end of racial policing, are disabled and still denied access to public spaces and services, or are young women still struggling with patriarchal attitudes and practices. (Roche and Tucker, 1997, p 5)

While the focus here is on young people, alienation is not the preserve of older youth. Feelings of alienation also impinge on younger children and can influence their perceptions of what society will offer them in turn.

Alienation also arises from the increasingly negative images that are presented of children and young people:

> [There is evidence that a growing] climate of suspicion, fear, and trepidation is fostered in which young people generally are the main objects. In a similar vein, analysis which highlights the relative powerlessness of young people and which speaks of 'this generation' as being victims, serves to call forth images and responses that welfarise the problem and pathologise the young. (Wyn and White, 1997, p 89)

The willingness of adults to pathologise even young children was clearly evident in the James Bulger case in 1993. James Bulger, aged three, was abducted from a shopping mall by two 10-year-old boys who subsequently killed him. The public response to the tragedy was indicative of the trend towards pathologising children. The case prompted an upsurge of public demand for punitive and repressive control of children emanating from an expressed belief that children were becoming increasingly violent. The Director of Barnardo's, replying to public reaction to the case, stated that there was no statistical evidence to support the perception of increased violence, arguing instead that the number of hard-core child offenders was falling (*The Observer*, 18 June 1995). Statistics, however, do not convince people, and it will be extremely difficult to shake public conviction that children and young people are becoming increasingly violent as long as the media continues to give prominent and sometimes exaggerated coverage to child crime.

Social exclusion and children

Over the last 20 years, the gap between rich and poor has increased more significantly in the UK than in any comparable country. As we discuss in Chapter 4, child poverty has worsened to a shocking extent: "It is clear that children, above all, are experiencing exclusion from full citizenship in the UK at the end of the twentieth century" (Daniel and Ivatts, 1998, p 74). Less attention has been devoted to the fact that children have born the brunt of a number of negative developments in public sector provision. These cutbacks have exacerbated the process of social exclusion. The issue of homelessness illustrates the point. In 1987 the number of households accepted by local authorities in England and Wales as homeless was 135,000 (more than double the 1979 number). Two thirds of these families had children. The situation became worse in the 1990s. The presence of young homeless people on the streets is readily apparent in most large cities. The equally serious problem of homelessness among younger children remains largely hidden as the children are 'provided for' in Bed & Breakfast accommodation. Living in temporary accommodation has a number of serious effects on a child's social and physical well-being, principally, restricted access to schools, healthcare and other public facilities. Furthermore, conditions in most temporary accommodation are less than ideal: overcrowded, poorly resourced, providing inadequate cooking, eating and bathing facilities and associated with significant levels of family stress. The continuing decline in provision of local authority housing means that the number of homeless children is expected to continue to rise.

In addition to cuts in housing provision there are a number of other areas where public service cuts impact particularly severely on children:

- *The decline in public transport:* this can be especially problematic for children in rural areas where cuts to public transport have been most severe.
- *Decline in health services:* children are one of the heaviest users of public health services. There have been cuts in public health services – in particular, the removal of local health centres and their amalgamation into larger often more geographically remote centres – which impact directly on children.
- *Cuts to public provision,* for example, parks, libraries, swimming pools, sports centres and the sale to developers of publicly owned land such as school grounds and sports fields.

Children reap limited benefits from a system of free market economics where competitiveness and cost recovery are prioritised. As 'minors' they are unable to directly influence decisions on public policy and spending. The issue of children's exclusion is further complicated by the fact that, even where facilities are ostensibly in the public domain, children's access to these public goods may be constrained.

The public domain

There is a noticeable trend of increasing adult intolerance of children, perhaps as a result of the growing number of adults who do not have direct responsibility for children. Lack of contact between adults and children can have significant negative repercussions for both. In their analysis of children in public places, Lennard and Crowhurst-Lennard grapple with the problems that children can experience as a result of reduced adult contact, asserting that children grow up unskilled in human relationships because so much of what needs to be learned cannot be learned only within the family or at school. They quote the planner Jane Jacobs to support the case for increased interaction:

> People must take a modicum of responsibility for each other even if they have no ties to each other ... this is a lesson nobody learns by being told. It is learned by the experience of having other people without ties of kinship or close friendship or formal responsibility to take a modicum of public responsibility for you. (Lennard and Crowhurst-Lennard, 1992, p 37)

Contact between children and adults outside the family is decreasing. Children are being increasingly removed from the public domain by parents worried about 'stranger danger' and other threats perceived as present outside the home environment. The message that the environment is dangerous is one emphasised by a number of organisations including the police and the Royal Society for the Prevention of Accidents: the message is that an unsupervised child is a child in danger. The result is that we have been panicked into conveying to our children the idea that danger always lurks outside the home. Parents are urged not to let their children out alone and to always know where they are.

Danger is not only the perceived 'stranger danger' but also the very real danger posed by the increase in car traffic, which has made local neighbourhood and main roads highly dangerous, even for the 'streetwise' child. Britain suffers from one of the worst child pedestrian fatality rates in Europe.

In assessing road accidents and the dangers of roads it is children who are inevitably seen as the problem. The emphasis in traffic management is on the child's behaviour as the 'cause' of accidents rather than the cause being that the car does not respond adequately to the child's presence. In the mid-1980s, Nottingham University conducted research which found that the position of children at the kerbside had no effect on the road positioning or the speed of the driver. The onus is on the child to see the car and react to it if he or she is to be safe, rather than the onus being on the driver of the car to see the child and react so as to ensure the safety of the child. It is a graphic illustration of what Qvortrup (1994) calls the 'adult praxis' at work, namely the right of the adult, the car driver, to have free access to the neighbourhood, despite the potentially harmful effect on children. The response expected of children is to stay away from roads and, where this is not possible, to give way to the car at all times. Children, therefore, are obliged to engage with society on adult terms, in an environment designed by adults and to cater for adults.

Children's ability to engage with their environment is further eroded by the predisposition towards intolerance of children's play activities in public places, even in places that appear to be designed for public use. This is indicated by the 'no ball games', 'no cycling' and more recently 'no skateboarding' and no 'rollerblading' signs erected at places where children may wish to partake of these activities. Banning these activities in certain public places does not mean that provision has to be made for providing public spaces where these activities may be legitimately practised. Even in places designated for public use, their use by children may be subject to constraints, as can be the case with public parks.

A large-scale survey of public park use observed 12,000 park users and found, as expected, that "public parks are a meeting place for young people." But they also found that "young people's use of parks is seen by other users and by managers as a problem" (Greenhaigh and Worpole, 1995, p 4). This negative attitude to young people, including children, was also identified in a study of a struggle over a neighbourhood park in London. Councillors announced that they were going to build a children's playground in the local park. In the process of developing the park two issues arose: the council's consultation with local people on the development was found to be wholly inadequate, and it was apparent that there was substantial antagonism to the park's use and perceived 'abuse' by young people. Further, "most people were not in favour of a playground ... the strongest objections came from people living in houses backing onto the park ... more than half did not want a toddler playground" (Craske, 1995, p 9). Instances such as this are not unique. They raise the serious question of where can children and young people express themselves? Which part of society and the environment can they legitimately lay claim to? How are they supposed to learn about their society and environment when they are so often excluded from its use?

Towards positive environmental relationships

Fortunately not all public perceptions of children and youth are so negative. Indeed, it is one of the great strengths of the move towards greater children's participation that attitudes that condone children's exclusion from the public realm are being increasingly challenged. Local Agenda 21, with its emphasis on involving children, has been particularly influential in this regard.

Children's integration into the adult realm is, however, a matter for debate and controversy. There are some who argue the case for children's separation from 'adult society' in order to protect the child from the excesses and demands of the adult world, to maintain and uphold the state of childhood. Postman is one of one of those arguing most strongly for a protected and separate state of childhood. He gives considerable attention to what he perceives as the dangers of eroding the line between childhood and adulthood (Postman, 1994). In exploring the case for increasing children's participation in planning for their community, it is necessary to remember that increased participation does not necessarily command universal support.

Children have a vested interest in their environment and in its improvement. This chapter has focused primarily on the problems children face in their environments, its inequities, constraints, issues of declining quality and children's exclusion from power and public places. Yet despite the seemingly overwhelming obstacles that confront children in their lives, opportunities are there and children are grasping them. Children are increasingly thrusting themselves forward and challenging the rights of adults to 'mess up' their future environment. As the Youth Statement from the UN Conference on Environment and Development in Rio (1992) clearly demonstrates, children and young people do not feel constrained by the term environment. They see it as an holistic term covering wider quality of life, socio-economic and political issues in addition to more specifically 'green' issues (see Table 1). This wider conception of environment is evident from research which seeks to identify what it is that matters to children (see Table 2). It is also apparent in the list of challenges which came out of the first children's conference organised by the UN (see Table 3).

The environment that children experience presents them with both challenges and opportunities. It is, as the brief appraisal of social demography, the economy, exclusion and other facets of children's lives examined here shows, one that in many ways is not conducive to children's position in the UK in the millennium. Nonetheless, it is the environment that children experience and it is an environment that, given the opportunity, they engage with forcefully – with understanding, compassion and zest. The challenge for decision makers is to understand children's lives and, through understanding and listening, to facilitate children's full participation in society.

Table 1: Concerns identified by children at the 1992 Rio conference

Black holes in Local Agenda 21 identified in the Youth Statement at the conference

- War and militarism
- Governance (new ways of governing the planet)
- Birth control
- Renewable energy
- Multinationals
- Refugees
- Nuclear disarmament
- Human rights
- Consumption
- Media

Source: Peace Child International (1994)

Table 2: Main concerns identified by children

Youth TGI (see Sparks, 1995) asked seven-year-olds what their main concerns were about the world today

Children's concerns	%
Drug taking	73
Cruelty to animals	72
AIDS	68
Dangers of smoking	61
Ozone layer	58
Unemployment	44

Table 3: 'Leave it to Us' children's conference

The international children's conference held at Eastbourne, England, in 1995 was the first international children's conference organised by the UN. It brought together 800 children from 83 countries. The children put forward a list of 26 challenges to be met by the people of the world.

Abbreviated list of the 26 challenges

1	We challenge airlines to use less packaging and to reuse plastic and materials that they use on flights and airplanes.
2	We challenge all governments of the world to spend a fair proportion of fuel tax on cycle lanes and cheaper means of transport.
3	We challenge all shops ... to stop using plastic bags.
4	We challenge the police to stop wrecking peaceful demonstrations.
5	We challenge all governments to make it easier to recycle plastic and to encourage manufacturers to cut down on packaging.
6	We challenge the English government to educate people about recycling.
7	We challenge France to consider the world when they test their nuclear experiments.
8	We challenge governments to give every person in the world the opportunity to recycle.
9	We challenge the governments to put laws against animal poaching and to put severe punishments for it.
10	We challenge governments to use money from tourism to take care of wildlife areas and endangered species.
11	We challenge governments to grow special forests on already cleared land for paper ... and to ban the import of rainforest timber for any purpose.
12	We challenge the governments to listen to anti-whaling groups and to pass a law against whalers.
13	We challenge all pet shops to inspect customers' homes and interview them before handing the animal over.
14	We challenge the governments of the world to ban importation of endangered species and to put some money into saving their habitat.
15	We challenge governments of the world to introduce more severe laws and punishments to penalise those who hunt endangered species.

Table 3: continued

16	We challenge the Brazilian government to encourage recycled material being used in construction.
17	We challenge all governments to provide cycle lanes ... to improve air quality, also companies to provide a bike or a transport ticket instead of cars.
18	We challenge shops to only sell cigarettes to those with identification to prove their age.
19	We challenge the governments of each country to learn how to be friendly to the environment.
20	We challenge the French government to stop testing nuclear bombs immediately.
21	We challenge the governments of the world to promote environmentally friendly alternative technology ... by doing this, jobs are created, which is good for economies everywhere.
22	We challenge the media to get together and form a children's media network.
23	We challenge the BBC to set up an educational series of videos on the environment for schoolchildren.
24	We challenge developers and architects to design affordable housing powered by renewable energy sources.
25	We challenge governments to supply most primary and middle schools with bins for recycling.
26	We challenge the UN to compel the governments to accept our challenges.

THREE

Children's rights

© The Children's Society

Growth of children's rights

The UN Convention on the Rights of the Child (1989) has received almost universal support. Within five years of coming into force it had been ratified by 177 of the world's 191 countries (Lansdown, 1995). A convention of such magnitude will inevitably impact on all aspects of children's lives – political, social, economic and cultural. It will also impact on those working with or on behalf of children. Professionals such as planners, architects, recreation managers, researchers and others who are involved with providing services that children and young people use will be required increasingly to take the articles of the Convention into account in carrying out their work

It has been suggested by some commentators (eg Newell, 1995) that the Convention is too distant from the lives of children in the UK to be effective. However, a campaign based on the Convention was sustained throughout the 1990s. The Children's Rights Development Unit

(CRDU) was set up in 1992 to promote the Convention's implementation. In addition to its campaigning, CRDU has worked on the idea of a national agenda for children, based on all the articles of the Convention. On the face of things, and certainly compared with the 1989 Children Act, the Convention has provided an important framework for promoting children's participation.

The working group charged with drafting the Convention had to consider how best to take account of children's differing circumstances and needs, and how to reflect the historical, economic, social and political contexts of the countries in which children live. It had to have relevance for countries with very different levels of development. It was a Convention that needed to address the life-threatening conditions facing children in many of the developing countries while simultaneously challenging the complacency of Western countries such as the UK. Children's rights also had to be addressed and articulated at different levels of responsibility: children, family, neighbourhood, local and central government, international governmental and non-governmental organisations. Despite the disparate circumstances and breadth of issues faced in developing the Convention, a common philosophy was identified. The underlying philosophy of the Convention is important in that it emphasises the need to always act in 'the best interests of the child'. It affirms children's rights to benefit from and participate in society on an equal basis. The preamble to the Convention states that children should be: "fully prepared to live an individual life in society and be brought up in the spirit of the ideals proclaimed in the Charter of the United Nations and in the spirit of peace, dignity, tolerance, freedom, equality and solidarity."

Four types of rights are identified in the Convention: survival, protection, provision and participation. These rights recognise and respond to children's needs and their powerlessness. They present a substantial challenge to all those who have responsibilities for children's welfare. Three of the Convention's 54 articles are particularly important as they provide the basis on which the other rights are built. These are:

Article 2: establishes that all rights identified must be available to all children and young people, without discrimination of any kind

Article 3: requires that in all actions concerning a child, the child's 'best interests' should be a primary consideration

Article 12: states that in all matters affecting them children and young people have a right to express their views.

These rights are far-reaching in scope, covering all areas of children's lives. In particular they have relevance for those responsible for the environments in which children live their lives. In the 1990s, environmental concerns have been high on political, economic and social agendas, with children's environmental situation being a dominant concern.

Children are at the forefront in the sustainability debate. As the World Commission on Environment and Development (1987) definition of sustainability states: "Sustainable development is ensuring that the needs of the present are met without compromising the ability of future generations to meet their needs." The lives of children of future generations require the adoption of a sustainable approach. Environmental mismanagement impacts particularly severely on children. It has substantial repercussions on their safety, health, mobility and development rights. Children's rights to a decent environment are enshrined in a number of articles in the Convention but most emphatically in Article 6, which calls on governments to ensure to the maximum extent possible "the survival and development of the child".

Children's rights are a particularly significant issue for developed countries such as the UK as it is the developed countries which are the profligate users of resources, producers of pollution and environmental degradation and whose life-styles are least sustainable. It is necessary, therefore, for governments, organisations, service providers and professionals to incorporate sustainability into their activities. Save the Children, for example, has committed itself to the support of local projects that are affordable and appropriate and sensitive to the local environment. There is also action being taken by and for children at regional and national levels. In 1999, 60 children from all over England presented their Action Plan to the Prime Minister, giving their ideas on how the government can help protect the planet. It was the outcome of the Children's Parliament on the Environment which is made up of 6- to 10-year-olds. The first priority identified by the children was to "ensure that we have clean air to breathe".

In addition to Article 6, there are a number of other articles in the Convention which relate directly to children's environmental rights and which architects, community workers, environmental educationalists, planners and other professionals can make use of in their work:

Article 24.2 (c): the duty to ensure the provision of adequate nutritious foods and clean drinking water, and to consider the dangers and risks of environmental pollution

Article 24.2 (e): the duty to ensure that parents have information and are supported in the use of basic knowledge relating to child health and nutrition, breast feeding, hygiene and environmental sanitation and accident prevention

Article 24.2 (f): the duty to develop preventative healthcare, guidance for parents, and family planning education and services

Article 29.1(e): the duty to ensure that education encourages respect for the natural environment

Article 31: the right to play, rest, leisure, recreation and participation in cultural and artistic activities.

The Convention is significant in that it affirms children's entitlements from society and what constitutes an adequate environment for children. It thrusts children's rights issues into a much greater range of professional and social contexts, challenging existing notions of social participation and environmental responsibility. It has the potential for bringing about substantial modifications in governmental and professional practice in any area where such practice impinges on children's 'best interests'. Strong feelings are raised in debates on children's rights where the lack of rights can be seen as a matter of grave injustice to children:

> In the 1980s and 1990s, approximately two million children have died in wars, between four and five million have been physically disabled, more than five million forced into refugee camps and more than twelve millions have been left homeless.... In 1994, over 22 per cent of all US children lived in poverty.... (Edmonds and Fernekes, 1996, p 1)

In discussing children's rights it is tempting to envisage them as something that applies 'over there', not to us in the developed West. As Lansdown warns:

> It is too easy to fall into the trap of believing that, as an industrialised, democratic society the provisions of the Convention are not relevant

> to us, that we already adequately care for all our children. The reality is that we do not. (Lansdown, 1995a, p 6)

The UK gives mixed messages on children's rights. On the one hand, it has hosted child-centred initiatives such as the international children's 'Leave it to Us' conference, held at Eastbourne in 1995. On the other hand, fundamental children's rights in the UK remain unmet and in some cases, as with increasing numbers of children living in poverty, their rights are being eroded. Children's rights need to be recognised as a critical issue:

- most children have no voice in major decisions that affect their lives;
- in 1995 4 million children were living in poverty;
- 150,000 young people are estimated to be homeless;
- physical violence and abuse of children is widespread;
- racial discrimination and harassment of children is a growing social problem;
- fear of traffic accidents and assaults on children has led to a significant reduction in the numbers of children going to school alone;
- children of unskilled workers are twice as likely to die before their first birthday as those whose parents are professionals;
- children living beside busy roads have a 50% higher chance of suffering respiratory problems.

UK and the Convention

Overall, UK governments have an indifferent record on children's rights, a record that has continued in the years following the signing of the Convention. The government ratified the Convention in 1991 subject to reservations, mainly concerning immigration, employment law and the detention of young offenders. In 1995, in fulfilment of its requirements under the Convention, the UK submitted its report to the UN Secretary-General in which it reviewed its progress on implementation. Lack of progress was observed in a number of areas, especially the increasing number of children living in poverty. The UN Committee recommended that the UK "undertake measures to make the provisions and principles of the Convention widely known to adults and children alike" (UNICEF, 1995, p 20). Under Article 12 the Committee suggested that "the state party consider the possibility of establishing further mechanisms to facilitate the participation of children in decisions affecting them, including within the family and the community." They are both criticisms that have especial resonance for the professions, many of whose members remain ignorant of the Convention and its relevance for their work and whose experience of children's participation remains minimal.

Criticisms of the UK's progress have also come from organisations within the UK, notably from CRDU, which concluded that "the UK is failing to comply fully with every single Article in the Convention ... it is evident that in many ways there is clear dissonance between society's professed commitments towards children, and the effective implementation of those commitments" (Lansdown, 1995a, p 113). The UK's failure is keenly felt by children, as a consultation exercise undertaken by CRDU found. Interviews were held with groups of children aged between 5 to 18 years who came from a wide variety of life experiences. The children shared a "powerful sense of frustration that their views and experiences were not being taken seriously at home, at school, by politicians, by policymakers and by politicians" (Lansdown, 1995b, p 14). These findings were echoed in the consultation exercise undertaken in our three groups. The Dunbartonshire group, for example, in commenting on their experiences with School Councils, felt that "most of the important decisions were already taken before reaching the School Council agenda, and whenever they had been involved in decision making it tended to be within narrow options or in areas that were so trivial that it was of no importance anyway". The Rochdale group, when asked whether children can form views and opinions that are relevant and coherent, questioned "whether people will listen" and pointed out that planners had "not even consulted adults". Therefore, while they are keen to be consulted, children are sceptical regarding the weight that will be given to their views.

If children's rights are to be meaningful, their basic rights need to be acknowledged and the culture of powerlessness and non-participation that prevails in much of British society must be acknowledged and addressed. As yet there are no effective mechanisms at either central or local government level for examining the impact of policies on children. In addition, responsibilities for children at both central and local level are divided between many different departments, often leading to a lack of coordination or integration of services. To achieve meaningful progress on children's rights it will be necessary, therefore, to focus attention on developing effective implementation mechanisms.

Articulating and responding to children's rights

Children, because of their age and their powerlessness with regard to resource allocation and decision making, are rarely able to articulate their own rights. They are dependent on others to articulate and service their needs. These needs are addressed by a number of organisations, service providers and professionals who, if they are serious about working with children, have to consider and develop mechanisms for addressing children's rights issues. The following are suggestions on how such issues may be approached, in particular, the process of enabling children's views to be heard.

Children's service providers and organisations

Compliance with Article 12 of the Convention would require all those who act as providers of children's services or who deal with issues that impact on children to:

- ensure that children have adequate information appropriate to their age with which to form opinions;
- provide children with real opportunities to express their views and explore options open to them;
- listen to those views and consider them with respect and seriousness and tell children how their views will be considered;
- let them know the outcome of any decision;
- provide children with access to independent advocacy;
- ensure that all guidance issuing from government departments on services for children reflects fully the principles of respect for children's views and their right to participate in decision making in line with their evolving capacity;
- sponsor public education programmes on the principles of the Convention and on the importance of respecting and listening to children's rights;
- ensure that training of all professionals working with children is founded on the principles of the Convention, and includes the development of skills in communicating with children;
- fund research on participation to be undertaken with children and young people;
- promote the introduction of structures within statutory services affecting children which seek to ensure children's participation in all aspects of the services (after Lansdown, 1995b, p 41).

Professions

Professions in the main, with the possible exception of architects, provide their services through the local authority. Thus it becomes imperative that local authority professionals understand the issue of children's rights and are able to take action. To address this issue the Association of Metropolitan Authorities (now part of the Local Government Association) and the CRDU produced a *Checklist for children*, which provides practical advice on the process of developing and monitoring policy and practice to ensure that it is in accord with the Convention (AMA/CRO, 1995). They identified a series of questions that the various professions should ask themselves. Examples of these questions are as follows:

- *Planners*
  How do you ensure development plans take adequate account of children's needs? (Article 3.1)
  How do you ensure that applications for planning permission for buildings show, where appropriate, that they include safety features and access and facilities for young children? (Article 3.1)
- *Architects*
  What schemes do you have for improving access and facilities for disabled children and young people in existing buildings and developments in line with Article 23?
- *Transport officers*
  What steps are you taking to develop a coordinated transport policy which takes account of the expressed needs of children and young people ... in line with Articles 6 and 12?
- *Environmental health officers*
  What procedures are you taking to minimise the risks of land pollution affecting children in your area? (Article 24.2 (c))

A potentially useful benefit resulting from professionals addressing seriously the question of how the implementation of children's rights affect them is to be more outward-looking. This point has been made about social workers:

> The opportunity presented by local corporate child care planning and strategies for youth, which offer a way forward for local implementation of the UN Convention, could assist social workers to review their familiarity with other professionals and volunteers

such as youth workers, advice workers, playleaders and community development workers. (Clifton and Hodgson, 1997, p 58)

Professionals and service providers are key to the provision of children's rights and to improving children's environments, but they cannot do this alone. Mechanisms need to be developed which provide them with information and training on children's rights, advice on how to take children's rights into account in their professional activities and guidance and support at both local and national level. Conversely, children need to know that mechanisms are in place to ensure that their rights are being supported, monitored and promoted by the professions and across all aspects of society. For example, the Rochdale children believed that children should have wider consultation before projects start as, "We feel that children are not aware of what is going on, regarding planning and building.... Once we have found out about plans they have already been completed and further consultation is not taken into account." It is a problem compounded by a lack of understanding of not only mechanisms but also of the role of the professions. This was clearly indicated by the children in Dunbartonshire who were able to discuss the role of teachers, youth workers and social workers in the context of decision making but not the role of planners or housing professionals which they did not understand. Children's rights, therefore, depend on both professionals and children having a mutual understanding of each other's roles and perspectives.

Mechanisms for promoting and monitoring children's rights

Several methods have been promoted by governments, local authorities and organisations for addressing children's rights: the appointment of children's ministers and children's commissioners, children's ombudspersons and children's rights officers and the promotion of children's charters. Although listed separately, the spheres of influence and responsibilities that are covered by these different appointments and mechanisms can and do overlap. When active they can provide vital information and advice on children's rights, implementation and best practice. They can also monitor not only overall adherence to and progress on the Convention on the Rights of the Child but on progress in government, local authorities, organisations, professions and service providers. The 1990s saw the development of a number of mechanisms for promoting, monitoring and guiding the implementation of children's rights. However, their influence has yet to permeate the work of professionals in areas such as planning, architecture and regeneration.

Children's commissioner

The appointment of a children's commissioner is one that has wide support, including support from the European Union, whose European Strategy for Children proposes a commissioner "having the powers and responsibilities necessary to bring about an improvement in children's lives" (Hodgkin and Newell, 1996, p 101). In the UK there is an active campaign for appointing a children's rights commissioner. Supporting organisations cover a wide range of interest groups. The lack of a children's rights representative at national level is seen by many as a major barrier to the promotion of children's rights. Children are the largest disenfranchised group in the UK (approximately 13 million). The primary functions of a commissioner for children would be to:

- instruct policy makers and practitioners to take greater account of children's and young people's rights and interests;
- promote compliance with the minimum standards set by the UN Convention on the Rights of the Child and other relevant treaties;
- ensure that children have effective means of redress when their rights are disregarded (Association for the Protection of All Children, undated).

In addition, the commissioner's powers would enable him or her to insist that government departments consult with the commissioner on any policy developments and legislation likely to affect children, to provide information on children's rights and interests, to monitor implementation of children's rights and to require responses to the commissioner's recommendations from central and local government, voluntary and private bodies.

Minister for children

In principle, a minister for children has much in common with a children's rights commissioner, namely a responsibility for improving children's lives and promoting children's rights. The difference lies in the institutional location of the two. The commissioner would act as an independent overseer, whereas the minister would work within government itself. Joan Lestor MP put forward a persuasive case for a minister who would redress the government's current pattern of behaviour where it "turns a blind eye to the realities of children's lives". She argued that "we need a political voice for children, a rights champion and much more information ... the overall objective should be to help make Britain more 'child-friendly' and to counter the fragmentation of services which currently exists in so many areas of service provision for children and young people" (Lestor, 1996, pp 103-4). An inquiry set up by the Gulbenkian Foundation into ways that central government could be improved for the benefit of children envisaged four main tasks of a minister for children:

- to develop and oversee a national children's strategy;
- to make children visible in government;
- to coordinate the work of government departments;
- to promote children's active participation in society (Hodgkin, 1998, pp 20-1).

The roles of commissioner and minister would be complementary, the minister would give children a voice in government and would promote the creation of child-friendly policies, while the commissioner would oversee the effectiveness of government policy in practice, monitoring and supporting the implementation and promotion of children's rights.

Children's Rights Development Unit

CRDU's work is organised around the fulfilment of three central principles:

- implementation of the Convention should apply equally to all children throughout the UK;
- the work of the Unit should be informed as fully as possible by the views and experiences of children and young people;
- the work of the Unit should be based on the widest possible consultation and collaboration with professionals, academics and other interested individuals (Lansdown, 1995a, p 108).

These three principles have resonance for the range of professionals whose support is essential for the implementation of children's rights. CRDU produces a range of literature on children's rights aimed at raising awareness and assisting with implementation, working both with professionals and interested parties and with children and young people themselves. It is especially concerned at what it perceives to be "a clear dissonance between society's professed commitment towards children and the effective implementation of those commitments" and the fact that "the views and opinions of children and young people are as yet given scant status and there is a prevailing perception of them as irresponsible, irrational and incapable of making informed choices" (Lansdown, 1995a, pp 113 and 117). CRDU has been effective in addressing these concerns and misconceptions and has made considerable progress in championing children's rights and encouraging organisations and professions to consider their relationship with children's rights. Its public register records indicate that by 1996 more than 400 organisations had signed up to the Convention.

Children's rights officers

Children's rights officers have grown markedly in number since the late 1980s, reflecting both growing concern regarding abuse of children's rights and, conversely, increased recognition of the need to promote children's rights. Officers are employed by local authorities. The work of children's rights officers has tended to focus on activities pertaining to social services rather than on wider activities across council departments. A broader remit, supported by necessary resources, could be one way of increasing the focus on children's rights within local authorities as a whole. These officers could also act as a valuable source of advice and contact for local professionals seeking to respond to children's rights issues in their work practices.

Children's charters

One method that has been used at various levels from international level to local level has been the adoption of charters. Charters are especially effective in focusing children's rights:

* *in particular locations*, for example, Children's Charter of Japan, 1951; Charter on the Rights and Welfare of the African Child, 1990;
* *with particular needs*, for example, Chailey Heritage Charter of Children's Rights (for disabled children), 1992; Charter of Rights for the Deaf, 1982;
* *on particular issues*, for example, Charter for Children's Play, 1992 (National Voluntary Council for Children's Play).

Charters represent an accessible and productive method that organisations, interest groups and professions can promote. They can be used to inform members of children's rights organisations and to offer guidance on the process of recognising and implementing children's rights. Charters offer positive benefits in that they can be adapted to meet the needs of the particular children involved and the particular focus of the organisation or profession. It is recommended that all professions, working through their professional bodies, eg RIBA (Royal Institute of British Architects), RTPI (Royal Town Planning Institute) and CIH (Chartered Institute of Housing) develop children's charters. These charters would signify a commitment to children's rights. They would also guide members in developing policies and practice that recognise and respect children's rights.

Implementing rights locally

The mechanisms summarised above depend upon national and local government decision making. Continuing to press for these is vital to planning with children for better communities. The concern of this book, however, is to demonstrate the need for professionals working locally, who do not necessarily have a specific brief to work with children, to do more to support children's participation. They are located in a range of professions – housing, regeneration, economic development, transport, community safety – and they are based predominantly, but not exclusively, in local authorities. They operate both as fieldworkers and managers.

The commitment of these professionals to children's participation has to be informed by the international and national framework on children's rights. At the same time, they need to initiate their own programmes and projects which, as will be argued in later chapters, relate to diverse communities. It is crucial for the issue of children's rights to be given meaning and reality – through local, mainly neighbourhood-based work – rather than for rights to be perceived as the domain solely of national campaigns and policy making. Accordingly, we end this chapter with a summary of a local project which addresses one of the most basic rights of children – not to live in poverty – through a participatory approach.

Child Poverty Project, Glasgow

The Child Poverty Project operates principally within the city of Glasgow. It has a small staff team employed by Barnardo's and is part of Barnardo's UK-wide anti-poverty initiative. However, it is run jointly with the organisation Stepping Stones in Scotland. Using a community development approach, the project works with children and families at neighbourhood level to identify child poverty issues. It aims to enable them to decide what to do about these things. The challenge for the project is to promote partnerships in which children and families can participate authentically alongside public and voluntary agencies. The main activities of the project have been:

* A Child Poverty Task Group to develop a shared understanding about what child poverty in one part of the city, Possilpark, meant in that community. This led to a participative research programme, the results of which were summarised in a booklet which highlighted children's play issues in the context of children's rights, child development and what was happening to the community. The booklet was used to provoke local debate on the issues and to build support for action. A campaign was begun to make play areas safer and some of the people involved set up a youth club.

* A recent development in the project's work has been its involvement in supporting the Commitments Task Group. Against a background of threatened council cuts, this group was set up to find out what families valued about the local family centre and to find ways of safeguarding these things for the future. (Wood, 1999)

FOUR

Children's participation and the political agenda

"As a group we feel that adults don't listen to us, due to our age and inexperience. We think they should consider a child's perspective on council projects and let us talk openly about our views, at an easily accessible point...." (Wardle Group)

"We've never been consulted...." (Bedford Group)

"Consultation should be honest. If young people are to be consulted there should be a determined effort to meet with them on their own ground and not to pre-judge or patronise them ... young people and adults should be working together, not against one another ... there needs to be greater effort from young people and adults to understand the other's point of view...." (Dunbartonshire Group)

Introduction

If children are to be active participants in their communities, and in the improvement of communities, they need to have available to them mechanisms and methods for accessing and influencing decision-making structures. The problem is that currently most mechanisms and methods are adult exclusive. As we enter the 21st century adult exclusivity is becoming increasingly challenged, both by organisations and agencies working with and on behalf of children and young people and by children and young people themselves.

In the 20th century a number of 'battles' against exclusivity were fought in Britain, notably the universal suffrage movement and the battles for equal rights for ethnic minorities, women, homosexuals, elderly people, for disabled people and those with special needs. Legislation has been mobilised to ensure that in law equal rights and equal opportunities for participation exist, even if in practice such participation, even for adults, is not well-established. There is, however, one notable group to whom equality of representation is denied, children, described by the Association for the Protection of All Children as "13 million citizens with no voice in government".

The direct representation of children in government, except through the appointment of adult representatives such as a children's minister, is unlikely to be realised in the near future, but at local level progress towards direct children's representation in local decision-making structures is being achieved. This chapter examines children's participation within the context of creating a social and political environment conducive to participation, and identifies the factors that both contribute to successful participation and some of the barriers that have to be overcome in its pursuit. Finally it offers some suggestions on the process of building participatory frameworks.

The case for participation

In developing her citizen participation model, Arnstein identified different levels at which citizens could participate in societal decision making, defining the aim of participation as follows:

> The redistribution of power that enables the have-not citizens, presently excluded from political and economic processes, to be deliberately included in the future.... In short it is the means by which they can induce significant social reform which enables them to share in the benefits of an affluent society (Arnstein, 1969, p 216)

It is a definition that is equally relevant for children's participation, the case for which is becoming increasingly well-established globally (see Hart, 1997). The arguments for encouraging participation are persuasive and can be summarised as follows:

- *Political case:* benefits accrue from involvement – services can be improved, representative democracy strengthened, and children and young people gain new opportunities, skills and insights (particularly relevant to professions and service providers);
- *Legal case:* under the Convention on the Rights of the Child, children have the right to participate (see Chapter 3);
- *Social case:* children and young people are members of society and share fundamental rights to participate with everyone else.

The right to have their say and be listened to is one that is continually expressed by children when questioned on what it is that they want from adults and service organisations. Research and surveys conducted across the globe support children's expressed right to be heard and to have a say in determining the future of their communities.

- In her survey for the UK's Local Government Information Unit, Willow found that: "Children and young people want to be listened to and involved. Whenever children and young people are asked what can be done to improve services, or local communities, they invariably suggest – listen more to what we have to say" (Willow, 1997, p 107).
- A survey of 45 groups of children aged 5-18 years by the Children's Rights Development Unit (CRDU) found that "common to all groups was a powerful sense of frustration that their views and experiences were not taken seriously at home and school, or by politicians, policy-makers and the media" (Lansdown, 1995b, p 14).
- *Rescue mission. A children's edition of Agenda 21*, which incorporates the contributions of 10,000 children, concludes: "Often we feel powerless. We think we cannot change anything until we grow up. Well, remember Samantha Smith: she helped end the Cold War with her letter to Andropov when she was only 10. Joan of Arc drove the English out of France before she was 19.... But this is not about child prodigies. The daily efforts of each one of us are at least as important. What matters is the voice of your heart. Let it be heard!" (Peace Child International, 1994, p 91).
- In New Zealand, Christchurch's Children's Strategy presents the following vision: "Imagine a city in which children are valued and precious – where politicians, children, parents, planners and business people move towards creating such a city. It would be safe. Children's opinions and perceptions would be given validity by decision makers."

For children's voices to be heard, society not only has to be willing to listen but also has to provide children with an environment conducive to speaking out.

© The Children's Society

Context for participation: social conditions and political exclusion

British society is characterised by widely differing levels and types of political engagement. It is an engagement that is influenced by social and economic factors such as class, poverty, education, profession, age and geographic location. Political engagement is socially and culturally determined, a determination that is clearly evident with regard to young people and which undeniably influences their willingness and ability to engage with existing political processes. Low levels of participation in national and local politics and across a range of decision-making processes in the UK is causing widespread concern both to policy makers and members of the public. One indicator of low participation levels generally is the fact that only just over 20% of people voted in the 1999 European elections. Whether this is due to general apathy or to more pervasive and deeper issues related to feelings of disconnectedness, and people's perceptions that decision-making structures are not relevant to them, is uncertain. What is more certain is that unless there is broad-based participation and social action in the community, the success of efforts to promote and support the participation of children and young people is likely to be limited. Children live in society, they imbibe its attitudes, practices and norms and learn by its example. If society does not value, and is not seen to be active in, political decision making, then why should they become involved? Even worse, if governments and local authorities are not seen to respond to adult ventures into the political realm then children may see efforts in this direction as futile and not worth engaging with.

Societal conditions influence markedly people's relationship with established political and decision-making structures. Young people have been particularly affected by the political and economic regimes and ideologies developed under the 1979-97 Conservative government. The move towards free market economics, competition and consumerism, and away from a more public welfare-oriented society, has impacted particularly on young people. In their analysis of youth and the economy, Wyn and White identify the impact of changing systems on young people, particularly the removal of many of the support mechanisms that were an integral part of the welfare state. Their focus is on Australia, but the message is equally applicable to British young people:

> The ideology of citizenship has shifted away from the rights of the citizen to universal social supports ... in its stead there is the view that citizens are best portrayed as 'consumers' of social services, and that the role of the state is to facilitate this consumption, preferably via the use of private providers ... this has enormous implications for how the state has responded to young people who have not been able to 'consume' the right way, to 'be responsible' in the appropriate

manner and to accept their duty as citizens to ensure the maintenance
of good order in the society at large. (Wyn and White, 1997, p 49)

Britain is experiencing increasing social polarisation, unemployment, homelessness and poverty. The curtailing of public support mechanisms such as student grants and housing benefits, and the replacement of apprenticeships with poorly paid and often exploitative youth employment schemes, have alienated many young people and their families. This situation has direct repercussions for participation:

> It is difficult for young people to 'fight' a system of which they may be a part, but from which they may feel totally excluded ... young people may find it difficult, and conceivably too confrontational, to criticise a social system in which they are not currently actively involved. They first need to join that social system (through participation within it) before adopting the possibly adversarial role encouraged by proponents of social action. Only then, as members of that society, are young people likely to share the power needed to influence change, in collaboration with other, more well established members. (Barry, 1996, p 11)

Analysis of the political culture and structures is, in short, an essential part of gauging the potential for children's participation. The extent to which children and young people were affected by the political, economic and social policies of the 1979-97 government remains an essential part of the context needing to be examined and understood. Britain became a much less equal society during this period, and children and families in deprived parts of the country became significantly poorer. The long-term impact of these changes will undoubtedly be shown to have been profound.

The Labour government elected in 1997, while intent upon carving out the middle ground of British politics, adopted a very different stance on the issue of poverty. Whereas the Conservatives were reluctant to recognise the existence of poverty, Labour put it at the top of its agenda. It replaced the term 'poverty' with that of 'social exclusion' and is seeking to use the latter concept as the core or lynchpin of its policies.

The Social Exclusion Unit, based in the Cabinet Office, has driven forward this approach in England. Similar developments have taken place in Wales, Scotland and Northern Ireland. In 1998, following the launch of its report *Bringing Britain together: A national strategy for neighbourhood renewal*, the Social Exclusion Unit set up 18 Policy Action

Teams to work on key issues. The teams produced recommendations during the following year and these have formed the basis of the government's strategy. At the same time, a series of related regeneration programmes (New Deal for Communities, Employment Zones), initiatives aimed at young children (Sure Start, Education Action Zones) and health (Health Action Zones) have been taken forward, all of them underlining the importance of community involvement. There are clear expectations that both funding programmes (Single Regeneration Budget) and local authorities (Best Value) will involve communities on a more substantive basis than before. The two key questions are: what does this actually mean? and what implications does it have for children's participation?

In one sense, the idea of social inclusion opens the way for community development and participation to become more widely recognised by policy makers and practitioners: "Inclusion gives a message of people joining in activities, debates and decision-making, not of being shut out" (Henderson, 1997b, p 9). However, there appear to be two assumptions contained within the government's commitment to combating social exclusion. One has to do with 'communitarian' notions of individual and collective self-help. This originates from Tony Blair's interest in the ideas of the American sociologist Etzioni, whose communitarian agenda includes a strong emphasis on social duties and moral responsibility, particularly with regard to the family (Henderson and Salmon, 1998). The other assumption is the equation made between social inclusion and employment. This can be seen most clearly in the priority given to vocational training and enterprise. The idea of lifelong learning and the learning society tends to be used in this sense too.

Caution is required, accordingly, when considering the potential for children's participation in Britain at the beginning of the 21st century. Blair is rightly applauded for being the first British Prime Minister to make a commitment to eradicating child poverty, but the route down which he has gone is at base strongly economistic and informed by powerful notions of family and community responsibility. These, on the one hand, often take the form of measures to control the lives of children and young people in communities and, on the other, suggest a formal and functional approach to participation (citizens' juries, 'compacts' between state bodies and voluntary and community organisations, an emphasis on consultation with communities rather than support for communities). Little awareness is shown of the genuine difficulties involved in supporting the participation of adults and children at neighbourhood level. On the other hand, the government's social inclusion agenda presents a real opportunity to strengthen the case for children's participation. We develop this point in the next chapter.

It is not surprising that in these conditions alternative youth sub-cultures develop with mandates characteristically different from those associated with the mainstream political agenda. Not only may the system itself be alienating but also attitudes to young people's participation can be contradictory. While the signing of the Convention, and the passing of the 1989 Children Act, indicate a commitment on the part of government to strengthening children's rights to be heard, conversely the 'illegal gatherings' definition within the 1998 Crime and Disorder Act is aimed directly at curtailing the activities of young people whose life-styles, behaviour and actions are seen to challenge the 'established order'.

Action has always been a core element in young people's political awareness. This action often focuses on issues which tend also to have an environmental agenda, issues such as nuclear weapons and, more recently, major road developments. The response of society to such environmentally-oriented social action is not always positive. When young people do raise their voices, as in the popular protests at Twyford Down and Manchester Airport and through the activities of groups such as Earth First, these are often seen by society as the extreme and threatening actions of disenchanted youth, rather than as action grounded on sound environmental principles. The reluctance to take these and other direct action initiatives seriously raises two critical questions: what is it about direct environmental action that gives it popular appeal to young people, and thus what is it about mainstream institutional processes that needs to be addressed if young people are to be encouraged to participate? To begin to answer the questions it is useful to explore the conditions necessary for successful participation.

Understanding and benefiting from participation

Participation is not a process that stands alone with reference to an identified group of children but derives from, and in turn impacts on, the wider society. Participation demands a commitment to listen and react to what comes out of children's participation, especially when such participation challenges the status quo.

Encouraging children's participation can also impact positively on the rest of society. The most obvious and possibly the most frequent examples of this process are associated with school-based environmental activities. These are activities such as building nature gardens, supporting recycling projects, initiating neighbourhood clean-ups and traffic campaigns focusing on roads near schools. All these activities usually require some degree of parental assistance. At a broader level there are examples of successful initiatives where children's participation has been part of a wider national environmental participation initiative, notably Local Agenda 21. Another example is from Sweden where the Q2000 Youth Campaign for Sustainable Participation, by involving governmental bodies, local municipalities, and making use of various community links, spreads the sustainability message beyond the youth community (Q2000, 1995).

Levels of participation

Concern has been expressed in many quarters at the high levels of non-participation of young adults. Increasing numbers of young people are not registering. At the younger end not only is there a lack of participation but in many cases the quality of children's experience of participation experience can be questioned. Participation requires that children understand the purpose of the participation, and have freely expressed their willingness to participate. Is planting a tree as part of a local restoration programme undertaken as a class activity, an activity that the child has freely chosen to participate in? Hart focuses on the different levels of participation based on his 'ladder of children's participation' (see Chapter 6). He also identifies simple principles that ensure an acceptable democratic level of participation applicable in any project (Hart, 1997). For children's participation to be successful there are a number of pre-conditions that have to be met: positive societal attitudes towards children's participation, the development of positive adult child relations in the participation process and a commitment to action. Table 4 summarises different ways of stating the pre-conditions.

Table 4: Principles and approaches to children's participation

Simple principles of democratic process (after Hart, 1997)	Local Government Information Unit's guidelines for involving children and young people in local government (after Willow, 1997)	Guidelines and considerations from Community Matters *Environmental Action Pack* on participation projects (1996)
• Children should understand the intentions of the project and have volunteered for the project after these principles have been explained • Organisational structure and power relations should be clear to all participants from the beginning • Rules should be established and amended by dialogue throughout the project • All children should have equal opportunity to participate • Bringing children in at the last minute is a classic error ... make the entire process of any project transparent to the participants • While not all children need to be equally involved in all phases, it is essential that, to the extent of their intellectual capacity, they are fully informed of the history and complete scope of the project and where they currently are in the process. No children should be excluding themselves because of a sense of incompetence	• Have clear objectives • Have clear boundaries about how much power and decision making will (or can) be shared with children and young people • Treat children and young people as individuals and acknowledge that not everyone will want to get involved • Take active steps to include children and young people not traditionally involved • Involve adults in a supportive or advisory capacity • Broadcast the benefits widely • Link general policies and strategies with particular projects and initiatives • Avoid looking for a single solution or a quick fix • Involve children and young people as early as possible • Constantly evaluate and learn from experience • Respond quickly to requests, prioritise informing them of outcomes and results	In considering how to involve children and young people in any environmental activity you need to consider: • how they will know that they have made a valuable contribution • how to overcome suspicion about any formal methods of involvement • how to ensure that they feel they will be listened to • the style and content of the information to be provided • how to involve them in the planning and running of the activity • how much control they should be given over the activity • health and safety implications • different approaches may be needed to reflect age, social class and ethnic differences

Overcoming societal prejudice

Children and young people's alienation from societal and political systems has been further increased by the tendency of adults to underestimate children's abilities to contribute to political and decision-making forums. This is illustrated in an honest report on a partnership initiative developed by Brecon Beacons National Park:

> The enthusiasm and honesty of the children in communicating their views to listening adults was encouraging and they seemed to enjoy the activities. The ease with which they understood how different people have different priorities for good reasons was unexpected; they were prepared to consider a range of viewpoints. (ERIC, 1997)

Children and young people can only show what they can do if they are given the necessary platform on which to perform. Many participation initiatives undertaken by organisations, in addition to recognising the positive benefits of these initiatives, often also express guilt at having underestimated the abilities of the children with whom the initiatives were undertaken. It is possible to overcome barriers, and in Table 5 we show how this can be done, enabling meaningful participation to take place.

Working together

Participation is not about adults withdrawing from the process and letting the children and young people 'get on with it'. Participation is about working together, with adults being there for the children as and when necessary, and as determined by the age, skills and other characteristics of the children concerned. Adult facilitation can be particularly important for disadvantaged children and youth:

> Young people on the whole do not want to 'go it alone'. Often paralysed into inaction by disadvantage and despair, many young people desperately seek the direction, authority, love, attention and encouragement of others whom they can trust in order to address the problems they face in their own backyards. (Barry, 1996, p 11)

Table 5: Overcoming barriers to children's participation

Potential barriers	Beyond the barriers
General culture of non-participation in society at large	Children's participation can encourage and act as a catalyst for wider participation
Lack of mechanisms for children's participation, in part due to the lack of any constitutional right to be consulted	The Convention on the Rights of the Child enshrines the child's right to participation. Increasingly local authorities are making commitments, either by signing up to the Convention or through Local Agenda 21. Mechanisms are being developed
Belief that children are not competent to participate in decision making	Examples of projects and work undertaken with children refute this notion
Imposing responsibilities can place unfair demands on children	The right to participate does not require participation. It has to be chosen freely
Rights are accompanied by responsibilities which children are not necessarily capable of meeting or may not want to meet	Responsibilities for children, as for adults, should be commensurate with abilities. Children will need to be provided with the wherewithal to carry out their responsibilities
Children's rights and demands may conflict, interfere with or detract from the needs of adults or other social groups	Children's rights are equal to the rights of others in society. A just society guarantees the rights of all its members.
Challenges adult relationships, especially parent, teacher and professional relations	Challenge and the reconsidering and reworking of existing relationships can lead to the development of more productive relations, providing these are based on mutual respect

A study of youth work projects from around the country found that the "single most important factor in these projects is the enthusiasm and commitment to the environment of the worker involved". Further, the research found that "you don't have to be an environmental expert to be a good youth worker – it is commitment rather than knowledge that is the essential ingredient" (Council for Environmental Education, 1995). It is a finding that should provide some relief to many venturing into the uncharted waters of both working with children and young people and engaging with new environmental issues.

Action/results

A commitment to action and results is something of which professionals such as planners, leisure managers, community workers – anyone engaged with children's participation – need to be aware. There has to be a commitment to ensuring that positive action follows from children's participation. Children need to see their efforts as valued and influential. For example:

> Children at Cross Flatts Primary school in Beeston in Leeds, working in partnership with a health project, identified the uncared-for appearance of Cross Flatts Park and its ever-present piles of dog mess as a major problem for their community. The children spent many hours addressing both these issues. They produced a booklet, made models of the park as it presently is and as they would like it to be (minus vandalised cars and dog mess), and had a public launch for their project to which councillors and other dignitaries were invited. If the children see that, despite their best efforts, there are no improvements in their park they will see their efforts as meaningless and so could be discouraged from any similar efforts in the future.

Participation must therefore come with a commitment to action on the part of those encouraging the participation, whether this be at national government, local authority or neighbourhood level. Non-action can lead to long-term disillusionment, a reluctance by children to engage further in environmental action and local decision making.

Successful participation thus demands a society which is committed to working with children and to providing a positive supportive environment within which to work. The second part of the equation is to develop methods conducive to ensuring that, when participation is undertaken, appropriate and productive means are used to achieve effective results.

Participation methods

Working with children presents local authorities and professionals with a number of challenges, not least of which is the fact that many local authority officers outside the social work and education professions will lack the skills, training and experience necessary for undertaking such work. For example, recreation planners may wish to involve children in the renovation of a local park and sports fields but they may not have the skills necessary to be able to undertake the process themselves. To achieve their goal the planners would have to work with, and be guided by, the skills of experienced child workers. In this case, the desired result of involving children may only be possible through partnership working, and by being open to the use of different time-scales, venues and methods. Fortunately, initiatives such as Local Agenda 21, City Vision and various regeneration initiatives have already created a climate in many local authorities and professions conducive to interdisciplinary and multi-professional working.

When working with children, professionals need to be aware that children may have limited understanding and patience regarding local authority and professional roles, structures, decision-making processes and time-scales. The development of more effective participation methods is something that local authorities and organisations are increasingly keen on developing, not least because they are a requirement of government and European funding regimes.

It is important that the organisations choose methods carefully and realise too that the principles of children's participation, that is, the need for participation to be active, interactive and 'hands on', can be equally relevant for adult participation. It is not just children who fail to respond positively to the 'meetings', surveys, and talking shop-type methods which typify many of the participatory programmes used by local authorities. There is a growing awareness of the need to use methods which put people at their ease and which go out of their way to involve participants in 'user-friendly' ways. Two methods developed to facilitate participation and which incorporate these principles are *Participatory Action Research* and *Planning for Real*. Both are methods that were developed for work with adults but which can be equally effective with children or with children and adults together:

> Recent debates about children's rights, and most notably children's role in the realisation of these rights, have prepared the ground for non-governmental organisations' inclination to extend the notion of grassroots to the children of the poor.... These factors have contributed to a growing interest in developing participatory action research methods that can be used with children. (Nieuwenhuys, 1997, p 234)

> Planning for Real is a consultation technique which encourages people to express their ideas about how they would like to see their local area developed. Using a large-scale model of the area and an

informal public meeting, Planning for Real exercises can combine first-hand local knowledge with expert advice from professionals. (Adams and Ingham, 1998, p 65)

The range of methods used in children's participation continues to grow. Some of them, such as conferences, partnerships and focus groups, mirror existing adult participation methods but with a children's focus, while others such as access days, children's councils and information exchange facilities respond specifically to the need for child-focused methods. Table 6 identifies some of the methods appropriate for use by local authorities and other organisations. There are a number of texts – Adams and Ingham (1998), Community Matters (1996), Willow (1997) which give fuller details on the range of methods that can be adopted and the strengths and weaknesses of these when used by participation projects.

Table 6: Methods for developing children's participation

Activity/ mechanism	Purpose	Example
Children's conferences	Opportunity for delegates to share ideas and projects and develop future directions and initiatives. Multi-media and video conferencing present further opportunities	International Children's Conference on the Environment, October 1995. Involved over 800 children from 83 countries
Surveys and consultation exercises	Obtain information and feedback necessary in developing child-aware services and structures	Manchester Children's Services Unit carried out a questionnaire survey with 2,000 children and young people, and interviews with 200, to assist the Unit in ensuring its services were best able to meet children's needs
Access days; Children's days	For a specified time each year, usually a day or a week, children's programmes are organised in which children's activities are prioritised and children are able to voice their concerns with leaders and officials at all levels of government	Manchester City Children's Week activities included a Children's Council, film festival, voting workshops with the Electoral Services Office, various sports, music and arts events, opening of the Town Hall, Central Library, Albert Square and other public centres to children's activities
Youth councils/ forums	Meetings of young people who come together, usually as a committee, to voice their views about their social and physical environments (Matthews and Limb, 1998)	Manningham Young People's Forum, set up after the Bradford unrest in 1995 to give a voice to young Asians aged 12-25
Newsletters, circulars and information leaflets	Promote information exchange, represent children's views and focus on subjects of interest to children	Children's Express, media project in London, in which 45 children aged 9-13 work as reporters on stories which are then placed in the mainstream media

Table 6: continued

Activity/ mechanism	Purpose	Example
Information exchange facilities	Place for young people to meet, obtain information and investigate opportunities for participation	Birmingham City Library Foyer
Partnerships	Combines the expertise, resources and experience of several partners to their mutual benefit	Sustainability for Real expanded the consultation processes used in its National Park Local Plan, creating partnerships between park authority officers, education officer, consultant, University of Hertfordshire, Royal Town Planning Institute, local schools and their pupils
Research	Acquire the data necessary for developing child-focused plans, strategies, policies and practice	Leeds Listens, research commissioned by the city council to understand more about how children and young people see the city and to explore their hopes. 2,000 children took part in the research
Action plans and strategies	Develop future plans and initiatives which reflect children's perspectives and needs	'York City Council: Our Future: A Plan for the Children and Young People of York.' Preparation included a two-day conference with professionals and young people
Focus groups	Where children come together with or without professionals to address particular issues	Safe Routes to School, a partnership initiative between four local authorities and Sustrans cycling organisation working with pupils in schools to help create conditions which encourage children to walk or cycle to school

© Ed Freeman

© Ed Freeman

FIVE

Children in the community

In the previous chapter we explored the potential for children's participation to gain a more significant purchase on the political agenda. In this chapter we move the telescope from the political to the community context. First we address the underlying questions: what are the preconditions or factors within communities which encourage children's participation? What is the contribution of community development to these processes and how can it be strengthened? Then we turn to the area of skills: *how* can children's participation in neighbourhoods be supported?

Experiences of community development

Over the last 10–15 years the range of professions involved in supporting work with and on behalf of children in communities has expanded. Once it was predominantly children's and play organisations which supported initiatives and employed staff; now they have been joined by housing associations, environmental organisations, local authorities, health authorities, community safety initiatives and others. It is important to identify key themes and practice models in the work supported by this range of organisations.

First of all, we must emphasise an obvious and simple point: work with and on behalf of children has been a significant part of generalist, multi-issue community development projects for more than 30 years. Children are members of communities as much as any other age, population or minority group and have the same right to be involved. In addition, adults' concern for children and their future has often been the springboard for community action. This characteristic of community development is explored by Hasler who identifies three approaches used by community work projects to the benefit of children and young people:

- face-to-face community work with children and young people;
- community work with local adults to the benefit of their own and other people's children;

- community work which is intergenerational and from which children benefit.

The extent of community involvement resulting from these approaches reflects the importance of children in community life:

> We often hear people say that the time when they have most friends in the neighbourhood is when they have children for whom they have to care. It may even be that children contribute to community life to an extent that far outweighs their numbers. (Hasler, 1995, p 171)

Accordingly, there are numerous examples of children's participation in each of the above three approaches:

- setting up play schemes and youth action groups with children and young people;
- tenants' and residents' associations advocating the need for safe play areas;
- community festivals which bring together children, young people and adults.

The investment of children in the areas where they live emerged strongly from the discussion groups set up in Rochdale, Bedford and Dunbartonshire to inform the content of this publication. On the one hand, the groups generated enthusiasm and suggestions for facilities; on the other hand, there was an undercurrent of resentment at the lack of consultation by adults when planning or intervening in communities in ways which directly affect children's lives. In Rochdale, for example, the group felt that, "children are not aware of what is going on regarding planning and building, especially houses on the green belt as this takes away our playing fields and our rural environment. Once we have found out about plans they have already been completed and further consultation is not taken into account."

In making the case to be listened to, children and young people are not usually arguing for their participation to be, as it were, fenced off from the participation of adults in community life. The conclusions of the Glasgow group at the end of their residential weekend were that:

- young people and adults are concerned about the same issues but from different perspectives and at different levels;

- young people and adults should be working together, not against one another;
- each has a tendency to 'stereotype'/'scapegoat' the other rather than address the real source of problems;
- there needs to be greater effort from young people and adults to understand the other's point of view.

This refutation of the divide between children and adults is an important theme throughout the book. It has to be understood as more than a challenging of the dependency of children on adults. Rather, it recognises the power held by adults in relation to children and seeks to turn it to the advantage of both: "Adults constrain children's choices ostensibly in the interests of children, but this can too readily become a rationalisation for marginalising children for the convenience of adults" (Hill and Tisdall, 1997, p 20).

The need to locate their work in local communities has been recognised by children's organisations, initially by voluntary organisations and more recently by local authorities. The emphasis placed on children's participation, reflecting the attention given to the UN Convention on the Rights of the Child, has not always been translated into community development, but on occasions it has done precisely that. This has been demonstrated by projects run by The Children's Society, Save the Children, Barnardo's and NCH Action for Children (Henderson, 1988; Callaghan and Dennis, 1997; Davis and Ridge, 1997; Save the Children, 1997; CDF, 1998) and by initiatives taken by some local authorities (Willow, 1997). Housing associations are an example of a sector which has engaged with the issue, placing it in the context of building effective partnerships (Wadhams, 1998). Many community projects supported by the Church of England's Church Urban Fund have also been committed to working with children.

Running through these and other projects is the belief that this way of working is effective. Hulyer, for example, in writing about work on two estates, believes that the benefit to children and their parents of after-school clubs, summer play schemes and play groups are self-evident: "Equally it can be seen that community associations, residents' associations and a community festival can benefit children and families through improving the area, or the housing" (Hulyer, 1997, p 193). A similar level of commitment informs the community work of many family centre staff and community workers, such as Bob Holman in Glasgow, whose work focuses on children and young people (Holman, 1997).

We are suggesting that work with and on behalf of children takes place in a high proportion of community development projects. In most cases it is implicit rather than explicit in that it is assumed to be part of good planning and practice. During the 1990s, it seems likely that this way of working became more difficult because of the tendency for regeneration agencies and partnership schemes to adopt a more targeted approach to working with communities. This is one of the criticisms of regeneration made by Henderson from a community development perspective. A breadth of vision, going beyond the terms set by planners and economists, is vital: "Nowhere is this more important than in work with and for children whose situation in neighbourhoods is affected by a number of forces." (Henderson, 1997a, p 25).

Yet the depth of experience of community development work which includes children should not be underestimated. In addition to the voluntary sector projects referred to above there is evidence that local authorities are giving it higher priority. Two examples of how commitment to community development and children at the level of the neighbourhood is strongly rooted are initiatives which are seeking to extend this form of practice by working on a city-wide basis:

In London, The Children's Society set up a partnership with five boroughs, Hammersmith and Fulham Urban Studies Centre and Planning Aid for London aimed at involving children and young people in local decision making, especially improvements to their neighbourhoods and school communities. The project team is able to use experiences obtained in different parts of the city to benefit particular neighbourhoods, all the time working closely with local organisations. The project leader's report on the first year states that, "In addition to the physical improvements and the provision of new facilities that children and young people have been involved in, the neighbourhood change has often a social dimension, improving their relationships with adults and between adults." (The Children's Society, 1997)

In Liverpool an initiative is being taken to promote the active citizenship of children through the setting up of a city-wide resource centre. The idea, which is being taken forward by The Children's Society, Save the Children and Liverpool Council of Voluntary Service, builds upon the considerable experience in the city of supporting children's participation at neighbourhood level. Particularly to be noted is the work of the

Liverpool 8 Children's Research Group, formed in 1993 under the auspices of The Children's Society. In the report of a conference held by the group in 1997, the need to link different initiatives was emphasised, bringing benefits of:

- greater unity in promoting children's rights and participation;
- the sharing of methods of working with children;
- enabling as wide an audience as possible to draw on results of work undertaken across Liverpool;
- the development of support networks and shared learning;
- assisting in identifying gaps in work with children;
- ensuring that future work is inclusive, representative of all children and addresses the issues of disability and learning difficulties;
- highlighting and celebrating the positive contribution that can be made by children.

(Liverpool 8 Children's Research Group, 1997)

Over the next few years, we may witness more initiatives which seek to move the practice of children and community development out of a wholly neighbourhood frame of reference. This relates to the recognition within community development that, while the energy and focus of the work needs to stay at the neighbourhood level or within communities of interest, there has to be a policy dimension to the work. There have to be mechanisms and staff within large organisations such as local authorities, health authorities and government agencies to help communities to have their voices heard and to ensure that government and European funding is allocated to community development.

The latter component of community development work has grown in significance in recent years – to the detriment of community development in the view of those who are concerned that community development is in danger of losing sight of its key objective of bringing about social change. In general, however, local authorities and other organisations which have seen the importance of having a strategic approach to community development and which have resourced it accordingly, are alert to this danger. Certainly there was a need to move away from equating community development only with grass-roots activity. It is a shift which has been broadly welcomed within the sector because it demonstrates community development's determination to engage with issues of policy, to be part of the mainstream rather than always pushed to the margins.

In summarising the contribution of community development to children's participation, it is fair to say that the policy dimension has still to be addressed in substantive terms. The London and Liverpool initiatives may point in that direction, and a small number of local authority children's services plans may include recognition of the issue, but there remains some way to go. It is possible that, as we discuss below, the government's social inclusion agenda, in which the future of all children figures so prominently, will have the effect of opening up the policy agenda. At this point, however, the judgement on community development and children must be: strong on neighbourhood work, weak on policy; considerable experience, knowledge and skills in the former, minimal experience, knowledge and skills in the latter.

Children and community development: the potential

Alongside the contribution of community development practice and policy to children's participation, a number of social policy issues can be identified which have the potential to support – even drive forward – children's participation. While the issues are often interrelated, we separate them out as follows.

Children and the community sector

There is a breadth of activities in which people can be involved at community level, ranging from community action to projects run by local voluntary organisations. The findings of a European research project provide important data on the number and types of groups and organisations to be found in communities (Chanan, 1992). The research findings were influential among both practitioners and policy makers in the UK and, during the 1990s, the term 'community sector' came increasingly into use to differentiate small, informal community organisations and networks from the paid voluntary sector. The implications for work with children in neighbourhoods is potentially considerable. This can be seen by reflecting on the functions, identified in the research, that groups carry out:

- organising *mutual aid* among people with a particular need, such as people looking after young children or elderly dependents;
- providing *social and recreational activities*, such as festivals, entertainments, sports;

- organising or campaigning for *improvements to the locality*, such as better services or new amenities;
- *liaising with authorities* and articulating needs and problems;
- providing *information, advice and assistance* on a particular social issue such as health, education or welfare;
- improving *employment opportunities* through training or enterprise;
- providing *local communications* such as a community newspaper or radio.

Groups may focus on only one or two of these functions, but often one type of activity will lead to another. It seems to us that both members of community groups and practitioners such as youth workers, planners, health workers and community workers could do much more to involve children in very local activities. The evidence of an active community sector provides the basis for this contention. The potential needs to be taken up. The government's compact with the voluntary and community sector provides a framework for this. It is 'a starting point not a conclusion' and a code of practice on children's participation could be drawn up.

Children, families and informal networks

The government's thinking is that the health and well-being of children and families is linked closely to the regeneration of neighbourhoods. A consultation document (Home Office, 1998) sets out a principle aim of strengthening the ways in which the wider family and communities 'support and nurture family life', and the Sure Start programme referred to in the previous chapter seeks to have projects serving the local community within 'pram pushing' distance. The initiative is being delivered through local partnerships with the aim of providing a range of support services, including childcare, early learning and play opportunities.

Within this part of government policy we can see some of the potential for the 'joined-up thinking' between departments and professions advocated by the government. It also builds upon the considerable experience and research findings on the role of family centres in deprived neighbourhoods, both as a resource for children and families and as a means of supporting informal community networks: 'a sense of community', gaining confidence and learning new skills have been important components of the 'neighbourhood' and community development types of family centre (Smith, 1993).

Whether childcare and protection policies can, within the framework of local authority social services, rediscover a neighbourhood aspect is more questionable. So powerful has the 'dominant discourse' about children become that it is hard to see a broader approach, one which links care for children with social exclusion, emerging. The phrase 'dominant discourse' is used by Moss and Petrie (1997) to explain the relationship between children, parents and society, and we return to it in the final chapter. Here we are pointing out that the discourse emphasises the extent to which – in the childcare setting – there is a tendency to categorise children as being essentially dependent and weak.

Regeneration and capacity building

The strong political commitment to involving communities in regeneration programmes is creating new opportunities for community groups. In England, the requirements of the Single Regeneration Budget and the New Deal for Communities embody this principal most obviously, but it is also explicit in policies in health, housing and the 'Best Value' of local authority services. Similar opportunities exist in Wales, Scotland and Northern Ireland. In a study of community participation in regeneration schemes, the authors point out that, "Communities can get involved in the regeneration of their own locality in a number of ways but regeneration programmes should always include work to build up and strengthen the natural organisations of the community itself. This is the central meaning of 'capacity building'" (Chanan and West, 1999, p 1). If capacity building is to be more than rhetoric and experienced as jargon by participants, it is vital that training and education become part of mainstream regeneration policy and practice. At present, provision is patchy and there is a need for a national framework which brings together the two areas of lifelong learning and regeneration (Henderson and Mayo, 1998). Including children in plans within the framework will be essential.

So far, both the wider issue of involving communities in regeneration and the specific issue of children's participation remains underdeveloped. One of the problems is the speed at which preparation of funding bids have to be made. This has caused problems for community groups because the pace of funding requirements does not match that of many groups: members need time to absorb information relating to the future of their community, groups have to meet and discuss. The opportunity, therefore, to involve children and young people in discussions about bids has been minimal. Yet the regeneration agenda is now so dominant in the policy context that, as we discuss in the following chapter, it is vital that ways are found for involving children and young people in both the planning and in the action which follows.

Social inclusion

One of the Policy Action Teams set up by the Social Exclusion Unit to take forward its report *Bringing Britain together: A national strategy for neighbourhood renewal* (1998) was on young people in poor neighbourhoods. The group's remit originally talked about 'youth disaffection', a term which the group was anxious to replace with something better. This suggests an awareness of the danger of labelling children and young people and, if acted upon, would have moved the group's assumptions closer to those made by community development. Even before the election of the 1997 government, many local authorities had increased significantly their commitment to anti-poverty work, combining action to ensure entitlement to benefits with a concern to increase opportunities for the involvement of poorer people in society.

Awareness of the danger of labelling children and young people and the significance of the anti-poverty agenda present major opportunities to push forward the issue of children's participation in neighbourhoods. They relate to the broader agenda of community development and social inclusion: "Knowing how to work with local people is the kernel of community development's contribution to social inclusion and citizenship. Its body of knowledge and skills, resting on a clear framework of values and principles, lies waiting to be understood and recognised in policy settings" (Henderson, 1997b, p 66). The underuse, to date, of a community development approach to including all children in society is a serious weakness. That is why attempts made in the media and elsewhere to demonise children in poor neighbourhoods need to be challenged. Going down that road, with its logic of curfews and similar control mechanisms, will have the effect of reinforcing the situations of children who currently come within the category of 'social exclusion'. Community development only works when it mobilises the positive interests and energies of people – children as well as adults. It has, therefore, to engage vigorously with the social inclusion agenda.

Sustainable development

We have noted already the growing concern and fears, among both adults and children, about the safety of children on Britain's streets and in public places. The combination of environmental and social factors is driving children out of neighbourhoods at the very time that children's concern for the environment is receiving wider global recognition. One of the participants at a children's conference held in Liverpool said:

> There's a big field and there's a wall around it and they won't let the children into it. They should knock it down, cut the grass and make a place for children to play. (Liverpool 8 Children's Research Group, 1997)

The need for support, at neighbourhood level, of this kind of awareness and commitment among children is crucial. The following are some of the resources:

- *schools* – environmental education projects can reach out into the community;
- *youth clubs and youth development groups* – detached and outreach work with children and young people who are either too young to belong to youth clubs or who are alienated from them;
- *churches, gurdwaras, mosques and other faith centres* – can offer meeting places and a range of activities within particular settings;
- *local voluntary organisations* – have members who provide a potential source of support for children's projects;
- *community groups* – can involve children in projects and activities;
- *local companies* – can often offer practical assistance;
- *local authority departments* – Local Agenda 21 units and leisure, education and housing departments have staff available to support activities and, in some situations, grants;
- *experiences of innovatory projects from elsewhere*, for example, on traffic calming, poverty and play.

The opportunities for supporting children's participation in environmental action need to be seized, alongside the strengthening of more practical, and practice-based, activities.

Skills for working in communities

In Chapter 4 we highlighted participation methods for working with children and young people. Here we specify the skills needed – mainly by professional practitioners – to apply methods effectively in work with adults. The focus is on the practitioner being 'close in' to neigbourhoods: the skills needed for direct, face-to-face work with local people rather than the organisational and policy skills needing to be used outside neighbourhoods to work on behalf of local people.

Our approach to this topic is twofold. Firstly, we think that the skills needed to work with local communities are shared by a number of different kinds of practitioners, among them community workers, youth workers, community-based adult educators, community educators, crime and drugs prevention workers and health workers. This is the realm of 'local educators' discussed by Smith (1994), practitioners working on a neighbourhood basis and making themselves highly accessible to residents. This is often expressed through street work, detached youth work and group work and the activities include problem solving, organising, campaigning, direct action, networking and adult education. There is a collection of skills which are generic and relevant to a wide range of practitioners. They need to be understood and used, for example, by planners, housing officers and regeneration staff.

Secondly, provided that practitioners draw in specialists to work with children and young people in particular settings (teachers, group workers, social workers), we think that the skills to which we are referring are as relevant to supporting children's participation as they are to working with adult residents on other issues. The proviso is important, particularly given the highly uncertain context of how adults and children relate to each other in public and professional settings, discussed in Chapter 1. The need for practitioners to negotiate how, where and when professionals will work with children, and who else they will involve, is paramount.

This imperative is captured by two practitioners who researched their work with children (4- to 11-year-olds), using schools, in a rural part of Cleveland. They were very alert to the degree to which they were working in a societal context in which children do not feel safe and valued:

> Planning research with this age group will take more time to manage issues of access and consent. It is important to make statements at all levels about confidentiality, child protection and use of findings. The planning of the actual fieldwork also needed very careful co-ordination between the workers and all participating schools, of timetables, children's groups and dates. This time was well spent and ensured the fieldwork went relatively smoothly. (Callaghan and Dennis, 1997, p 9)

Adopting this approach will be an essential part of good practice in all other settings in which work with children is being planned – play work, consultations on planning proposals, involvement in regeneration schemes and so on. The attention given to careful negotiation with parents, adults and the children involved will need to be undertaken carefully and sensitively and with clarity about the details of arrangements.

Having set out the above dual approach, we now outline the set of skills associated with the methods for supporting children's participation. The following framework is focused on the role of the professional worker – it is not being suggested that it can be applied to the actual activities of community groups. It will be seen that it places an emphasis on planning carefully any work that it is to be carried out in neighbourhoods and on being very specific about the tasks to be undertaken. In the following chapter we identify key skills required to work directly with children

The neighbourhood work process

1   Planning and negotiating entry
The skills needed here will already be familiar to professional planners: being clear about the role you are going to take in and with the community and making initial contact with key community groups, voluntary organisations and statutory agencies. Letting people know who you are, and what your broad intentions are, will provide a basis for establishing mutual trust.

2   Getting to know the community
Collecting accurate information about a community – its history, its economy, housing and other resources, its organisations and facilities – is an essential part of neighbourhood work. Key to handling this area successfully is being clear *why* particular data is to be collected, what you and your organisation need to know and how you propose to collect the data.

3   Working out what to do next
A more detailed planning phase is needed to assess likely problems and issues, to set goals and priorities and to specify what precisely is going to be done.

4 Making contacts and bringing people together

Making contact with key individuals and organisations in a neighbourhood gives a signal that neighbourhood work is being undertaken, and bringing people together in small, informal groups demonstrates the kind of work that is intended. There are several ways of making contact in neighbourhoods, and choosing which methods to use will be influenced by the nature of the community as well as the skills and resources of professional staff.

5 Forming and building organisations

The shift from having contact with individuals and small groups in a neighbourhood to establishing and working with a properly constituted community group is a major step. It commits both professionals and members of a group to responsibilities of a different order to those of an informal group.

6 Helping to clarify goals and priorities

Most community groups need considerable support in being clear about what it is they are seeking to achieve and in making choices about what they will concentrate on first. That is why this aspect of neighbourhood work is identified. Getting this bit right is often the key to a group's success.

7 Keeping the organisation going

After initial enthusiasm and activity a community group can often experience a loss of energy and direction. It is at this point that a practitioner needs to be on hand to provide a different kind of support and to help members plan for the long term.

8 Relating to other organisations

The focus of a community group tends to be mainly on building its own organisation and networks. Fairly soon, however, it will need to establish links with other organisations, particularly the local authority and regeneration agencies. Here members need to be helped to be effective at negotiating and at demonstrating a group's competence to others.

9 Leavings and endings

A professional worker will not be able to provide support to a group for ever. And in many situations it may be appropriate for a group, once it has achieved its objectives, to end. In both of these situations it is important to manage leavings and endings properly.

(Henderson and Thomas, 1987)

The above nine stages constitute a process, a series of stages which can help practitioners to plan their interventions in communities. It should not be understood as a strictly linear process, only moving onto a new stage once the existing one has been completed. Working in neighbourhoods is more complicated than that – activities and tasks merge with each other, often in quite challenging ways. This is particularly true for work undertaken by adults with and on behalf of children because this is an area about which people tend to hold strong opinions. Helping them use their energies effectively, for the benefit of children, is vitally important and calls upon a range of skills in each stage of the neighbourhood work process. In addition, evaluation of what is being done needs to be part of each stage of the process, thereby helping the practitioner to review plans and change direction. Using the above framework will only make sense if the watchword throughout is *flexibility*.

SIX

Children and professionals

This chapter reviews the overall context in which professional groups accommodate the voices and needs of children. It uses the categories of professions identified in Chapter 1 as a framework in which to assess the perceptions towards them of children, referring to the material obtained during the three consultation exercises with children. The key questions that we consider include:

- Why should professionals be interested in children's perspectives?
- What can professionals learn from a child's perspective?
- How can they gain access to a child's perspective?

It concludes with a series of observations and recommendations for good practice, referring where appropriate to actual examples.

The context: worlds of working with children

"The toddlers are the bicycles, the children are cars, the teenagers are vans and the grown-ups are the lorries."

At first sight this seems a somewhat off-the-wall remark: whatever does it have to do with children and their interaction with different groups of professionals? It actually refers to a family conversation taking place in one of the author's cars as she and her family returned from a brisk walk in the North Yorkshire countryside: "a wobbly cyclist veered across our path, and a heated debate followed as to which methods of transport should assume priority on the road. The statement of hierarchy voiced by my daughter encapsulates neatly her metaphor for how she sees power distributed in our society, with adults firmly in control!"

If the metaphor is transferred to the world of work where we begin to question and debate the extent to which professionals are the juggernauts and trucks cutting up the cars (and presumably failing to see the bicycles at all), we can see the extent to which the interaction between professionals and children is often fraught with difficulties.

The Chartered Institute of Housing argues that devising strategies for allowing children's voices to be heard is not straightforward and calls for a good understanding of how children think! (see *Housing*, February 1999). While this sounds oversimplistic, it is important to realise that this kind of common sense is not typical and is rarely grasped by the range of professionals whose roles involve engagement if not directly with children, then with the issues, policies and practices that will have some impact on children's lives. For it raises the question of whether 'professional people' have any in-built or pre-ordained ability to communicate with children. Probably not, for it "is only in recent years that the insights of those who have made deep study into the needs of children have trickled into everyday practice" (Ross, 1996, p 91).

Different groups of professionals have very differently constructed relationships with children, some formally and legally constructed, and others far more loosely defined, so here we comment on the implications of these different 'levels' of involvement. It has been noted that, broadly speaking, we can divide up the professionals involved with children into two main groups (Dwivedi and Varma, 1996). First there are those who engage with children as part of a specific referral service. This includes social workers, educational psychologists, child psychiatrists and family therapists (in some instances the police could be located in this category).

Then there are the professionals who children meet in the usual courses of their lives, whether on a regular or occasional basis. This group can be further sub-divided, into those whose regular contact with children is more obvious and formalised and includes teachers, health visitors, general practitioners, youth and play workers, and those whose professions are not generally associated with working with children. This includes housing officers, planners, children via school-based projects or developments within their neighbourhoods, particularly those who live in areas undergoing regeneration. Different professions will have varying amounts of contact with children, and the nature of the relationship between professional and child will vary depending on the situation.

This book is primarily directed towards those whose contact is less common and who are unlikely to have had any specific training on working with children. Much of the literature on policy and practice around child interaction and participation emanates from the first professional sphere outlined above, and education disciplines, but there are themes and strands that cut across sectoral boundaries to have a wider deployment: "The attitudes and practices of professionals are the product of a variety of factors. In addition to their psychological background and 'baggage', and their professional training and experiences, the concerns of the State and their cultural ideologies also exert a very important influence" (Dwivedi and Varma, 1996, p 3).

The concept of 'independence' highlights this breadth of influence. The overwhelming cultural ideology in Western societies is to promote and encourage independence in children as early as possible – consider the toy shops which market themselves as 'Early Learning Centres' rather than retailers of play equipment: a series of disguised influences is operational here. But the desire to promote independence, especially by parents, is sometimes merely an *illusion* of independence. To what extent do professionals aim at encouraging independent views and opinions so that children *appear* to have their own voices? And when children's voices are in opposition to parents, and professionals, does this create the illusion that they are *really* independent, and rebellion and non-conformity become proxies for independent behaviour?

The focus on polarity and difference is not necessarily productive, for when consulting with children "shared expectations and general atmospheres are deeply effective in bringing about success or failure" (Cullingford, 1992, p 144). Children are not a race apart, they are just as influenced by their society as other people and "it is not as if they see the adult world as separate and of no interest to them. On the contrary, they show such interest that they struggle hard to make sense of it in their own way. But they are not helped or encouraged. In the absence of analysis, tone is crucial" (Cullingford, 1992, p 147). Children's natural and acquired abilities to reflect and empathise with other people's points of view are often underestimated, and that they need to further enhance these abilities by participation and negotiation is ignored, or at least not developed in any rigorous way.

Professional reluctance

In the professional world it is unlikely that the audience is entirely in agreement that a child has a right to be heard, and there is not necessarily a commitment to the notion that a child's perspective on an issue is always relevant or vital to its resolution. One of the most predictable barriers is that adults, especially professionals, are inclined to be anxious or to show resistance when a child is not perceived to be exercising *power* appropriately. How professionals interact with and on behalf of children is subject to a wide range of influences. On the one hand, they can be the product of professional training, but on the other, they may also be the result of more general societal attitudes towards children. Both these areas of potential barriers appear to contribute towards a level of mythology about the nature of children's abilities and capabilities which serves to disguise their actual potential for involvement in service planning across different professional domains.

Children are assumed to lack responsibility, interest and experience. Is this because we rely so much on a model of childhood, with its roots on 19th century thinking, which treats all children as immature and irrational? Or is it that they are treated as byproducts of other units of study such as families or households? These assumptions become transformed into real obstacles, for children are *not* given responsibility, their experience is *not* validated and they are *not* generally allowed to become interested in adult activities. A note of caution is needed, however – these obstacles should not be allowed to mask real issues that must always be considered when working with children:

- managing issues of access and consent;
- child protection issues: professionals need to be very clear about relevant laws, policies and procedures;
- confidentiality;
- management of the use of findings from doing research with and consulting children.

Overall, however, our experience during the course of researching this book was of the wariness displayed by professionals in developing good practice in planning with children.

Professional responsibilities

The fundamental reason why professionals should be interested in children's perspectives rests on the principle that public bodies have a responsibility towards all their citizens, whatever their age. New approaches to government and governance must reflect ideas of inclusiveness and participation. The work carried out by the Social Exclusion Unit on school exclusion and truancy has raised issues of 'joined-up government': the need for coordination and communication between all relevant departments. The multiplicity of statutory plans that are currently affecting children necessitates better information sharing between professionals and, indeed, appropriate training to produce better understanding of interprofessional issues affecting children. There is some evidence that perceptions towards children are gradually changing. There is an emergent consensus that, "given the correct circumstances children enjoy being asked, are enthusiastic and keen to participate if the subject matter is relevant to their lives. Children will happily engage in activities which stretch their imagination, allow space for creativity and incorporate an element of self-determination" (Callaghan and Dennis, 1997, p 44). In the local authority/housing association field there is a growing awareness of the need to try out a variety of particular techniques with children, although there is no agreement on the most successful strategies.

The reasons why professionals should be interested in and sensitive to children's perspectives across a whole range of issues are discussed in Chapter 4 and can be summarised as follows:

- children are members of society in their own right and therefore have a basic right to be involved in matters that affect them;
- children use most, if not all, the public services and so can offer informed opinions about their experiences of them;
- sometimes children know things that adults don't about issues and can offer a perspective that may have been overlooked;
- involvement improves relationships between adults and children as it is likely to break down real and imaginary barriers;
- children's participation can improve services by bringing new or revised perspectives;
- children learn to respect others through being respected for their opinions and contributions;
- children can learn about democratic processes and citizenship at an early age through direct experience.

What can professionals learn from a child's perspective?

In this section we describe and analyse how children view their relationships with key professionals. We do this by reflecting on a general model of participation and consider distinctions and differences between and within professional groups. In the Scottish consultation with children carried out for this book the children identified a ladder of degrees of participation which adult professionals could choose to utilise. We acknowledge the debt to Arnstein (1969) and Hart (1997) in this construction and note that, while the ladder of participation concept may be somewhat overworked, this one was devised by children themselves and shows how astutely children perceive professionals' attitudes towards them, particularly where involvement and consultation are issues. It is important to mention that projects can have elements working at a number of the levels; for example, children may be involved in a project at level 6 but the good work is undone when children are ignored in presenting results or in deciding allocation of resources which, regardless of children's concerns, are then overridden by budgetary constraints or other agendas. This is illustrated by children's involvement in the Manchester bid for the Olympic Games 2004, which began at around level 6 but ended at 0.

Children and professionals: a ladder of participation

10 *Children in charge:* children decide what to do. Adults only get involved if children ask for help
9   *Children lead/adults help:* children take the lead in deciding with help from adults
8   *Joint decisions:* adults and children decide together on a basis of equality
7   *Consultation:* adults consult children and consider their opinions carefully, then adults decide taking all opinions into account
6   *Invitation:* adults invite children's ideas, but make the decisions themselves on their own terms
5   *Tokenism:* adults decide what to do. Afterwards children are allowed to decide some minor aspects
4   *Decoration:* adults decide what to do. Children take part by singing, dancing or performing ceremonial functions
3   *Manipulation:* adults decide what to do and ask children if they agree (children must agree)
2   *Adults rule kindly:* adults make all the decisions. Children are told what to do and given reasons and explanations
1   *Adults rule:* adults make all decisions. Children are told nothing except what they must do
0   *No consideration:* children are not given any help or consideration at all. They are ignored

In Chapter 1 we identified a series of categories of professionals and we now expand on these and comment on how they are perceived by children. So we comment first in general terms, exploring professions and the nature of professionalism generally, together with the implications of 'professional politics' and the role of locally elected members. We then briefly consider 'child-centred professionals', that is, teachers and social workers. The category of programme staff includes regeneration officers and partnership staff, which will include architects, surveyors and related development staff and tenant participation workers. We then shift our focus to the grass-roots practitioners whose influence is increasing: community workers, youth workers, playworkers, drug prevention staff and arts workers. Finally we discuss service delivery professionals from planning, housing and health sector backgrounds.

Professionals generally and elected members

The children involved in the consultations showed a tendency to lump together a mass of decision makers that included teachers, councillors and officials. Their overall recommendation was that professionals should rethink their consultation methods to be more sympathetic and appropriate to young people as a target group. They were able to link their specific feelings and experiences into a more strategic context and equated their feelings of detachment from decision-making processes to more general equalities issues. Children appeared to feel strongly that we do *not* live in an equal opportunities society and some reported endemic sexism and racism.

The Wardle Group, during the production of their children's charter, came to the conclusion that "we feel that adults don't listen to us, due to our age and our inexperience". The local council appeared far removed from their world and there was a perception that it was not interested in their needs. According to the Group, "We think they should consider a child's perspective on council projects and let us talk openly about our views, at an easily accessible point, eg a 'surgery' for children as well as adults. It could be attached to a youth group, preventing intimidation and adding strength to a point of view." The Wardle children and young people felt that they did not have open access to local government, for while they feel that a level of access is there, they "are discriminated against, eg if you go to the Town Hall and an adult is next to you he will see the adult and listen to the adult", "decisions are made on financial gain". To illustrate this, the children cited the example of a local cinema for which they campaigned but failed to keep open. It was replaced by an out-of-town multiplex which is not accessible to children.

Interestingly and positively, all children in the three groups focused on self-responsibility: that children should make themselves better informed and more organised, so contradicting the popular belief that children are neither independent nor interested.

Child-centred professionals – teachers and social workers

Distinct hostility was shown towards teachers because children saw little opportunity to significantly influence policy or practice at school. Arguably, the comments directed towards teachers and social workers were predictable, because of the roles assigned to them by society. There was, however, recognition of improvements in this situation as children progress through school (privilege of age); this is perhaps symptomatic of general attitudes towards children's abilities and their potential for accepting responsibilities. Lack of respect from teachers in general was cited, with examples of the most important decisions being taken before reaching the agendas of School Councils. Where they were involved in decision making it was in areas that were trivial and of no importance.

Responses referred to authoritarianism, negative attitudes and disrespect, but it was acknowledged that these exist within the context of quite restrictive official boundaries. Social workers came in for considerable criticism, partly because their work was understood in pathological terms: being assigned a social worker was indicative of being a *problem*, and young people felt that they were rewarded for being as normal as possible. Social workers were not seen as helpful in solving problems but as fostering dependency, not preparing children to live in the real word. Social workers were felt to treat children with more respect if the child had an adult or support worker with them.

Programme staff and grass-roots practitioners

The participating groups of children had little to say about programme staff, appearing to have had little connection with any of these professionals. Concern was expressed by the Wardle Group that children living in areas undergoing regeneration were considered at the expense of those who did not live in what they perceived to be deprived areas. However, this range of professionals remained, for the most part, anonymous.

Attitudes to grass-roots practitioners, on the other hand, particularly youth workers, were very positive. Youth workers were seen to be friendly and helpful, approachable and providers of accurate advice. A few, however, were not seen as willing to listen, and some areas of importance were open to the discretion of individual workers. The positive associations with this category of professionals suggests that they may be well placed to be instrumental in the development of better and permanent avenues of consultation with other professionals.

Service delivery

This was an area where children's understanding and familiarity were patchy and often dependent on their experiences within their families. Children have very limited experience of the role or work of housing professionals and need help in understanding the housing system and their first experience of this sector. However, they expressed an awareness of conflict on housing allocations over, for example, anti-social tenants, issues around the curtailment of local authority housebuilding programmes and difficulties in agreeing priorities.

The fact that children showed awareness of housing issues augurs well for the development of better links with this profession. Indeed, providers of social housing in particular are generally closer to the communities they serve than any other profession in this category. Many local authorities and housing associations already employ community or tenants/resident participation workers, in contrast with, for example, planning or economic development departments. Resident involvement in decision making is an important performance indicator for registered social landlords and there is growing evidence of an extension of this principle to include children and young people. If housing is to assume increased importance in regeneration programmes this marks a real opportunity for progress (see Chapter 7).

The children who participated in the research demonstrated very little contact with planning professionals and had very scant understanding of their role or functions. It was evident that they had not been involved in any planning consultation and that development proposals had not generated any publicity to attract children. On the other hand, the respondents grasped the concept of 'Not In My Backyard' (NIMBYism) and related it to specific unpopular projects. Children would appear to distinguish planners from other professional groups. Planning is clearly an important arena where consultation should be seen to happen. The children did not feel that any concerted effort to achieve this had ever been made, citing finding things out by chance and reading little bits in local newspapers as being the key ways of gaining information. Yet children were aware of the benefits of being involved in planning issues.

So we now ask the question, how can professionals gain access to children's perspectives? What individual and collective skills and structures are needed to facilitate this shift in focus? By what means can professionals develop effective ways of involving children?

Developing skills to maximise children's participation

In the final section of the previous chapter we specified the skill areas needed to work with adults in communities. Some of these are transferable to work with children, but clearly there are also some for working specifically with children. Pugh and Rouse-Selleck have identified a framework within which to debate this, and we use their criteria as a basis for our discussion (Pugh and Rouse-Selleck, 1996).

Key skill: *Professionals need to develop expectations of children appropriate to their age and level of understanding.*
The children in our case studies agreed strongly that they can form views and opinions that are relevant and coherent, "but they are not always listened to." Children have a valid and vital contribution to make – that is the expectation which professionals should start with. For example, in 1999 Leeds City Council won joint first prize in a national competition to enable local authorities to showcase the best aspects of their work. A 15-minute video entitled *Seen and Not Heard* was devised and produced by a group of teenagers representing the city's children, demonstrating just how children are able to influence the decision-making processes in the city. This was facilitated by youth workers but drew on key projects from a range of professional domains.

Key skill: *The ability to listen reflectively so that consideration is given to assessment and planning opportunities.*
Involving children in planning "provides information to planners about children's use and perception of the environment so that children's own needs are better planned for" (Hart, 1997, pp 74-5). Leeds City Council has coopted eight children onto its Young Persons Strategy Steering Group with the intention that elected members on this panel will be advised by the very people who have first-hand experience of children's issues. Manchester City Council's Planning Department actively involved children in the preparation of its Local Agenda 21 strategy, using a series of mechanisms to ensure that children's voices were not just heard, but acknowledged and regarded.

Key skill*: The ability to see things from a child's view.*
Although we have all been children we should acknowledge both that our memories may not be an accurate reflection of our experiences and that the rapid pace of change has transformed the daily lives of children. Members of the School of Art, Architecture and Design at Leeds Metropolitan University introduce the child's perspective to their students. Aspiring architects have worked on projects (within school settings) in places as diverse as the market town of Wetherby and the inner-city area of Hunslet, devising play areas with extensive design input from the users themselves: an effective way of seeing things from children's perspectives.

Key skill: *The ability to observe and interpret children's representations.*
The case study children asserted that:

> "...adults and children's needs are basically the same but it is how they are treated in obtaining what they need that is the difference. There is a communication problem because children are not treated as seriously as an adult should be in the same situation. This is why there is such a strong 'borderline' between the decision makers and the young whom the decision will concern." (Wardle children)

Workers from a community project on the Hawksworth Estate in West Leeds, an area of relatively low demand for housing characterised by high incidences of anti-social behaviour and perceived youth disorder, used a youth forum to design and carry out an estate survey which was intended to pinpoint key areas for improvements to the neighbourhood. Such a simple device provides a means for children to put forward their opinions.

Key skill*: The ability to extend children's thinking, in terms of the skills of listening, negotiating, reflecting and observing.*
These all need to be modelled and supported by adults. Children themselves acknowledge that they should be willing to take up opportunities and be aware of them; to educate themselves and become less discriminating. Professionals have the capacity to support children in this enabling process and it is an important skill to develop. Media professionals have been successful in this area with the establishment of two British bureaux for Children's Express, the international news agency run by children. The Newcastle bureau was opened in 1997 after its staff had been trained by teenage members of the London bureau.

London members have presented reports to the Cabinet Office, participated in television and radio broadcasts and run seminars. Supported by adult professionals, they have assumed primary responsibility for all aspects of their concern.

Key skill: *The ability to be respectful, accepting and patient.*
Respondents in the case studies felt that involving young people also means letting them know what is happening in a language they understand, not patronising them, or giving up when they do not understand planners' or council language. Professionals need to acknowledge that children are not all stereotypes. They have their own individual opinions. In 1997, Women in Design and Construction, a Leeds-based group, obtained National Lottery funding to examine the role of art in strengthening community spirit and sense of place, and a key objective was that it should grow out of the community and be as participatory as possible. Rather than identifying children as a separate group in the process, their opinions and responses were built in at every stage of the preparation and delivery: they were successfully 'mainstreamed' as a natural and important element of the community. This demonstrates respect of children by adults.

Key skill: *The ability to help children to express and manage their feelings, including anger.*
Adults need to be able to hear children's voices of resistance and protest. One issue that provoked a very emotive response from the Bedford Group was that of 'a healthy environment', to which the response was "healthy England – Ha! Ha!" And in response to being asked what young people need to do, said "write even more letters, but who listens or reads anything from us?" Protest from children is as valid as that from adults and should not be confused with rebellion and alienation.

These key skills are not exclusive to any particular profession. They are, in fact, what human resource professionals describe as 'soft skills', and are relevant in a wide variety of professional and personal contexts. These skills are increasingly considered to be key competences and needed by practitioners and managers across a range of professions. Yet many new entrants to the professions we have discussed in this chapter have had little or no development in these areas. Communicating, listening, problem solving and empathising are as important for professionals as academic qualifications. In many organisations, excellent 'customer service' skills are a prerequisite for many staff: for professionals to engage successfully with children the development of these 'soft skills' needs to assume a higher priority in training strategies.

Professionals working together with children: the way forward

We now draw together the main issues in this chapter and examine the potential of different strategies for advancement. Some professional bodies, such as the Royal Town Planning Institute (RTPI) and the Royal Institute of British Architects (RIBA), have education units to serve as a resource to their respective professions and provide the necessary materials for children doing school projects. Similarly, the Chartered Institute of Housing (CIH) produces an interactive education pack which helps children become aware of the different housing options available to them as they become young adults. Education, however, does not equate with participation. It is not a consultative process and is less about involving children in the democratic process and more a resource for other purposes. Our main interest and concern is the way in which professionals interact with children on a day-to-day basis. The CIH has instituted a series of *Good practice* guides for involving children in the consultation and decision-making processes associated with the work of registered social landlords, and it is the CIH guidelines that form our framework for the conclusion of this chapter.

Do we need to improve the image of professions?

It has to be acknowledged that some professionals carry either a dull or poor image. This was borne out by the responses of the case study children. The issue needs to be addressed for a number of reasons, not least so that professions become more accessible and user-friendly to children. The key factors needed to improve the image of a profession are listed as follows.

Outreach work

Children engaging with representatives of certain professions may incur the derision of their peers. Possible ways of overcoming this can include reaching out to meet children on their own ground and making sure that children are encouraged to believe that they have their own contribution to make to whatever the issue may be. The very practice of consulting with children may in itself be self-reinforcing and self-validating. For example, the Bedford children recommended that professionals should coordinate a 'participation and empowerment scheme' which would involve explaining how to influence 'the system', assisting in the selection of a full-time representative who can be in touch with young people. Birmingham City Council Housing Department has put this into action and employs a worker whose remit is solely working with children living in properties and estates managed by the local authority. This includes encouraging participation in decisions ranging from the provision of leisure facilities to decisions about how their homes are managed and by whom.

Flexibility

There needs to be flexibility, a willingness to amend strategies as children's priorities become apparent: "... communicating with children is a different matter from being kind to or fond of them, or being very skilled at coping with their physical needs" (Ross, 1996, p 92).

Pluralism

It is important to be aware that different groups of children want different things depending not only on their age but also their cultural background and ethnic identity. This is a key reason why a multi-agency approach is essential. Children are not an homogenous mass.

Resources

The costs associated with developing professional expertise, staff resources and networking to work more closely with children may seem high. Yet the costs of not addressing children's needs are likely to be even higher in terms of children's alienation from 'officialdom' and disenchantment with democratic processes. In the context of the debate on social exclusion, willingness to invest resources in supporting children's participation must be a priority.

Underpinning these ways of improving the image of professions as far as children are concerned must be some essential strategic rules of good practice.

Race and gender

The hazards facing professionals meeting children if they have not thought about issues of gender or race will be severe. It will mean that communication is blocked. There is a danger too, in the context of seeing children themselves as dangerous, of responding only to boys and using very traditional methods of alerting and maintaining interest.

Incentives?

The traditional mechanisms whereby professionals attempt to draw people in can be counterproductive. Most children find well-tried methods and mechanisms, such as meetings and questionnaires, off-putting. They are more likely to respond to appropriate incentives to get involved. This can simply be a matter of where to convene. For example, Cadwyn Housing Association in Wales used a local McDonalds restaurant to hold meetings with children, using the lure of free food. The Children's Jury at Grimethorpe, South Yorkshire, was offered the opportunity to work away from home, in pleasant and comfortable surroundings, reflecting the value placed on the project.

Research the issues

Children will respond enthusiastically if what they are being invited to respond to interests them. This calls for preparation and groundwork in terms of setting out an agenda for children's consultation. Again, surveys will be more effective if they are done in partnership with a specific youth organisation. Liverpool Housing Trust used a specialist group called Action and Adventure to devise a questionnaire for children which raised their profile in the area. The process of consultation was as valuable as the findings.

Education

While we have sought to keep education and participation separate, the contribution of education to children's participation is clearly vital. In the environmental field especially, education about issues can have a positive effect if it is couched in terms that are relevant to children. Birmingham City Council's Housing Education Officer, for example, helps children make their own videos on estates in order to identify specific problems such as those associated with traffic. Although an educative process, it is a form of participation in that children's opinions and ideas are given voice and made explicit. The Children's Society and other childcare voluntary organisations have also pioneered similar estate-based work with children.

Monitoring and evaluation

Encouraging and developing children's participation will be time-consuming and costly and is likely to have operational implications for professionals. Encouraging children's participation will also affect the work done by any particular organisation. It is important, therefore, that professionals are clear about performance and progress in this area. There are a number of options:

• awareness of the issues of working with children can be incorporated as a learning outcome in professional education, in the same way as resident involvement is studied on housing courses;

• this aspect of work can form part of service delivery strategies, with quantifiable objectives. The responsibility can lie with individuals, or teams, or be allocated to a specific individual as part of his or her duties.

There are other ways of ensuring that professionals' work with children is monitored and evaluated and none are mutually exclusive. Our concern at this point is to highlight the issue.

Concluding comments

In this chapter we have drawn attention to the key questions that are involved in the way different professionals engage with children, emphasising some of the difficulties and barriers that are not necessarily evident when working with other sections of the community. In doing so, we have set out to demystify the feelings and responses of children, who all too often are seen as dangerous and problematic. Children are as varied in their characters and aptitudes as any other section of the community but have not been afforded the same rights and respect as the adults they share their lives with. There are opportunities for professionals from a wide range of disciplines to develop their skills and competences in a two-way process which can only benefit themselves and children alike.

SEVEN

Involving children in regeneration

An example of a professional working with children in neighbourhoods.
© The Children's Society

Urban regeneration in the UK and other European countries assumed enormous significance throughout the 1990s and provided many opportunities for interprofessional cooperation and collaboration. However, the impact of participation by local communities in regeneration has been varied, and the involvement of children within those communities has often been left to chance.

In this chapter we offer an overview of regeneration policies in the UK and examine attempts by different agencies to involve children and young people in the design and implementation of regeneration. Using community participation and networking theories as a framework, we identify appropriate opportunities for developing child-friendly regeneration policies and processes. This involves a review of the various different approaches to regeneration prevailing at different times and commenting on the position and role of children in areas which, prior to regeneration, are often associated with the concept of social exclusion. We draw particularly on the material gathered during the Scottish case study prepared for this book to establish preliminary models for children's participation in urban regeneration.

How can we define regeneration?

At its most literal definition, to regenerate implies "to undergo or cause to undergo moral, spiritual or physical renewal or invigoration: to form or be formed again" (Collins English Dictionary). This is not an inappropriate definition in the context of urban regeneration, because the themes of social (as opposed to moral), physical and economic renewal are interrelated and inseparable strands. Neighbourhood regeneration has been defined as a product of structural changes that have occurred in regional economies which are themselves influenced by changes in national and global economies (Thake, 1995). We must bear in mind, however, that regeneration cannot be described or defined as a standard process because different regions have different problems and require different approaches to tackling them. But, overall, contemporary regeneration is identifiable with a strategic focus of implementing strategies to 'turn around' those areas which have above-average indicators of deprivation, and which are seen by both the local community and outside agencies as needing action to rebuild confidence (Taylor, 1995). Regeneration, therefore, has become an all-encompassing word used to describe a range of initiatives and processes, all of which impact on the communities which experience them.

The background to regeneration in Britain

Regeneration of specific neighbourhoods or areas is a complex process with a varied history in terms of the success of its intended outcomes. Here we trace its development over recent decades and highlight important policy shifts. Regeneration-type activities in the UK since the end of the Second World War have been well documented (McKay and Cox, 1979; Sills et al, 1988; Talbot, 1988; Atkinson and Moon, 1994). Improving the conditions, whether these be social, economic or physical, of people living in deprived areas (usually but by no means exclusively urban) has been a matter of concern, if not for action, for successive governments.

Regeneration as a phrase was coined in the 1970s. It was borrowed from the USA where its focus was on the use of private money developers to lever in investment. In the UK, although regeneration only entered popular discourse in the 1990s, regeneration has existed as a concept in a series of guises which can be traced back to the 1960s. The first regeneration activities emerged from 1968 onwards with the Urban Programme and the Community Development Projects. These initiatives were viewed with a certain amount of suspicion by central and local government because of their overtly Marxist content. They were significant because they marked a clear departure from purely physical responses to perceived problems typified by inter- and post-war slum clearance programmes. The Urban Programme was designed specifically to regenerate areas. The 1977 White Paper was a key turning point in the change from a social pathology to a structural understanding of poverty. It marked a move from the notion that, because of the comprehensive nature of the welfare state, residual poverty could be explained by the pathological behaviour of those people or communities who remained in poverty, to an approach which located 'regeneration' in a wider context (Atkinson and Moon, 1994). This paved the way for communities' involvement in the regeneration of their own areas.

These tentative steps towards community regeneration suffered a serious setback in the early period of 1979-97 Conservative rule, for Thatcherism did not espouse the philosophies and ideals associated with this concept. However, there was growing realisation that the massive cost of urban decay needed addressing urgently and this underpinned the move towards the ambiguous but popular concept of partnership: public/private alliances underpinned by sound economic development. Enterprise culture was the panacea that would underpin moral as well as physical and economic regeneration. During the years of Conservative rule, the Department of the Environment (now the Department of the Environment, Transport and the Regions) retained its role as the key government department for regeneration and assumed responsibility for a multitude of programmes and initiatives, most of which were designed to encourage private investors to return to the cities.

The opportunity here for the genuine empowerment and involvement of communities was unclear. Certainly the private sector has a role to play, but what actually occurred was a heavy reliance on property-led regeneration, on flagship projects. It has been suggested that the creation of long-term mechanisms to benefit real people was largely ignored. City Challenge alone stood out as significant in that it required the participation of local communities in the development of approved projects (de Groot, 1992). While each regeneration initiative had its own funding and eligibility criteria, as well as its specific aims and objectives, all of them were underpinned by the philosophy that government should not play a lead role in regeneration, and that the "spark of regeneration must come from within the inner cities themselves" (DoE, 1988, p 5). What emerged was a picture of considerable incoherence and contradiction as a result of the apparent reluctance to "attempt to define the focus of activity" (Atkinson and Moon, 1994, p 165). Indeed, "government support programmes [were] seen as a patchwork quilt of complexity and idiosyncrasy.... The rules of the game seem over-complex and sometimes capricious. They encourage compartmentalised policy approaches rather than a coherent strategy" (Audit Commission, 1989, p 1).

Regeneration into the millennium

Regeneration of urban areas was addressed with renewed vigour throughout the 1990s. The Single Regeneration Budget (SRB) was introduced in 1994 and represented a combination of 20 separate programmes. Its key aim, to act as a catalyst for regeneration, is supported by three basic principles:

- the importance of partnerships: to address the complex nature of deprivation and disadvantage;
- the spur of competition: to ensure value for money and the approval of appropriate schemes;
- a hands-off management approach: to ensure the needs of the community are not subsumed.

We can characterise SRB as imposing a four-pronged attack on selected areas of deprivation, in which social and community issues are placed high on the agenda as one of the key objectives. Figure 1 identifies the main elements of this approach:

Figure 1: The four-pronged attack: dimensions of regeneration

- Enhancing the physical condition of targeted areas
- Taking measures to stimulate the local economy
- Tackling social and community issues
- Establishing a long-term vision: strengthening the potential for self-government and sustainability.

Source: After Skelcher et al (1996)

It would appear that SRB has been embraced with few changes by the Labour government, although the competitive element has been watered down. In practical terms, interim assessments indicated a wide variety of community involvement, and this resulted in a series of directives that local communities must be more involved than ever. This represents an attempt to redress the fact that communities have generally been bypassed in regeneration decision making. Ten per cent of Round 5 of SRB monies were to be allocated to fund capacity building, that is, developing skills in the community. At the same time, a series of 'Pathfinder' examples were selected to implement schemes under the 'New Deal for Communities' programme. The notion of community is assuming primacy.

Community involvement in regeneration

We have established that current thinking about regeneration highlights the importance of community involvement, but how in reality should this happen? The community should be involved as consultees, as participants, as partners, and the level of involvement is indeed used as an indicator to measure success. In this chapter we do not attempt to explain why community involvement is important. We would, however, stress that, because it is accepted as useful and essential, it is necessary to consider all members of the community. Community involvement in regeneration can be applied at a range of levels and for a range of purposes. Figure 2 sets out discrete elements of this overall process and establishes a hierarchy of participation, beginning with the role of recipient and ending with that of partner.

Figure 2: Five roles for the involvement of the community in regeneration

- Beneficiaries of the programme and users of services (personal and social development; youth crime prevention)
- Consultees and representatives of local opinion
- A source of general community activity which in itself has an economic value
- A source of organisation which can help to deliver parts of the regeneration programme and generate community economic development
- Potential long-term partners in regeneration.

Source: CDF (1997)

There is a long and well-documented history of community participation, particularly among tenants of residential social landlords. It is important to acknowledge, however, that this track record of participation and involvement has remained within a somewhat rigid professional and political arena: it is by no means certain that the competence and organisational capacity of local community residents is given equal weighting to the contribution of public authorities and other partnership agencies. Furthermore, there is a real danger of community interests being sucked into formal structures (Stewart and Taylor, 1995). Indeed, community involvement and rhetoric often go hand in hand. We cannot assume that partnerships will lead to the empowerment of local people. Indeed, there is a danger of community members of partnership bodies being dominated by agencies:

> A crucial issue for the effectiveness of partnerships in tackling poverty and social exclusion is the limited degree to which many local partnerships appear to be making 'partnership with the community' a reality. (Geddes, 1997, p 115)

In any discussion of community involvement, therefore, it is essential to pose key questions:
- How best can residents be approached and engaged?
- How should involvement be organised?
- How can effective working relationships be created?

These are challenging questions in any circumstances, and are made even more so when applied to children.

Participation for children

It is possible to specify how adults can be part of the process of selecting, planning and carrying out projects, with the ultimate aim of empowerment, equality, reciprocity and mutual respect (Flekkoy and Kaufman, 1997). Children's participation has similarities, but it also has differences, and this is why it is seen as problematic. Indeed the actions of children and youth are often viewed as contradicting the process of developing responsible citizenship and sustainable environments!

There are relatively few examples of the involvement of children in the regeneration process and the establishment of sustainable and successful schemes in which children have been active in driving the process. Where children are engaged they will need to be supported in the gradual development of their autonomy and self-reliance and generally will need more guidance. They are still dependent, to a greater or lesser extent, on adult support. As a result, the level and complexity of their involvement needs to be tailored to suit their maturity. The question is, how? It may be that for children, the less formal mechanism of the voice is the only realistic option for participation. Formal structures can impede participation.

At this point we move away from the preoccupation with structures for participation and focus more on networks as appropriate, informal mechanisms for participation. This dimension is backed up by the requirement that bids for SRB funding/programme delivery should highlight the role and level of involvement of community and voluntary networks. It is useful to apply the questions on community involvement posed above to the role of children's participation and to link them with the role and purpose of networks. Networks are assuming a greater significance in regeneration because they are "organised to enable individual participants to make connections with one another without the necessity for meetings or rigid procedures" (Gilchrist, 1995, p 32). Networks allow enthusiasm and experience to cross boundaries, skirting round the traditional barriers that exist within most regeneration arenas. Networking also affords the opportunity for empowerment, particularly among those sections of the community who are often excluded from mainstream participation methods. Figure 3 illustrates how networks can be employed to fulfil a number of purposes to support key community-related activities within the context of regeneration. In terms of the presence and participation in the process of networking, evidence suggests that children remain confined within the 'linking' sphere.

Figure 3: Purposes of networking

- *Linking:* using networks as a mechanism for facilitating communication between interested parties
- *Supporting:* networks as a means of support and reinforcement; this implies a more active role
- *Managing:* networks as a mechanism for managing a process, as opposed to more formal, official structures
- *Application of skills:* networks as forums for the sharing and application of skills appropriate to the process of regeneration

Source: After Skelcher et al (1996)

The case for engaging with the issue of children's involvement in regeneration is being strenthened from a number of perspectives. Research, for example, is beginning to acknowledge the importance of neighbourhood for children and by association their role in changing neighbourhoods (Brookins et al, 1997). It is likely, therefore, that demands on planners, designers, environmental managers and other professionals involved in regeneration will increase as they become more concerned with children's needs.

In suggesting that networking is an effective way of empowering children in the regeneration process, we need to be aware that empowerment is an emotive and problematic term. Any analysis of empowerment has to ask *who* is disempowered, and if so, whether this is systematic or not. May's analysis of gender and regeneration can usefully be extended to children. How do they internalise their own low social status? How can this be turned around? These issues of power and exclusion need to be understood, because one of the more destructive reactions to disempowerment is that of internalisation, with a consequent loss of self-esteem and of any sense of ownership, that is, the "power to make a difference to one's own life or to that of the community" (May, 1997, p 27). Power structures can easily become accepted or internalised without question or recognition: children face many barriers which exclude them from the processes of empowerment. It is also worth introducing a note of caution here because empowering and enfranchising children can lead to an unwelcome blurring of the category of childhood itself (Jenks, 1996). Should children be allowed to be just that, or should they be prepared for formal structures as early as possible? In general, the exclusion of children from processes of empowerment and participation can only increase the likelihood of long-term alienation. At the same time, exclusion means that the social and community benefits of children's participation are lost.

How does regeneration relate to the concept of social exclusion?

In Chapter 4 we introduced and examined the concept of social exclusion and its application to children's lives. We return to this topical issue in the context of regeneration, for when considering the impact of regeneration it is also important to acknowledge the context of deprivation and disadvantage which triggers the need for regeneration-type activities. Inequalities in the distribution of wealth clearly have a major impact on where regeneration takes place: we can say with a degree of accuracy that areas in need of regeneration are synonymous with indicators of social exclusion. Too often regeneration areas are characterised by run-down, unpopular swathes of local authority housing, whether it be traditional house styles or high density, system-built flats and maisonettes.

We have described how the substance of regeneration in the UK appears to be a catch-all for a series of physical, economic, social and environmental improvements to an area which are intended to redress the processes that have led to a state of social exclusion, of detachment from the mainstream developments and activities of everyday life. We know the extent to which social conditions impact on the ways children use and value their environment. Children need places with clear spatial and social identities. Children living in overcrowded conditions usually find ways of extending their territory into semi-public and public places (Bannerjee and Lynch, 1977). There appear to be close links between social exclusion and the amount of disruptive behaviour in deprived communities and this highlights the perceived impact of social conditions on children's lives. The Social Landlords Working Group on Crime and Nuisance has an officer responsible for developing and promoting strategies to 'contain' the behaviour of young people, particularly in the public or social rented housing sector. This fits in with the overwhelming notion that it is children who need to adapt their behaviour to suit the environment rather than adults looking for a solution which enables environments to be adapted to enhance children's physical and mental well-being. A pilot child curfew scheme in Scotland in early 1998 was seen to reduce local crime: police in South Lanarkshire reported that crime involving under-16s had dropped by one third during the period of the curfew and complaints about youth disorder had dropped by half. Local politicians described the success in terms of removing the oppressive climate of fear. Police forces across the country considered the practical implications of introducing schemes to remove children from the streets at night. Media reporting suggests that public opinion in the UK in general is negative towards children and there are high levels of fear of children among adults.

It is, of course, much easier to define what damages and spoils communities rather than what makes them work, and children in deprived urban areas are easily stereotyped, despite being regular victims of crime themselves: "In general, today's inner-city youth are seen as being at risk of a host of negative developmental outcomes" including crime, educational deficit and the absence of fathers (Brookins et al, 1997, p 47). Yet we need to consider the impact of making the correlation between regeneration areas and high concentrations of 'dysfunctional families' condemned to spawn a new generation of disaffected youth. This can only contribute to the stigmatisation of children. Furthermore, fixed perceptions about the nature and role of children lead to difficulties at a practical level. For example, part of the environmental improvement work on a SRB-funded Leeds scheme included provision for children's play spaces, and this seemingly straightforward issue at once revealed tensions and conflicts. These included:

- What was an appropriate level of provision? Different interest groups want provision for different age ranges with by far the least contentious group being the under-8s. These pose the least threat, and their needs are likely to be most associated with being with adult carers.
- What was the likely nuisance impact of the different groups of young people (particularly those who acted independently of carers)? The conventional participation methods used tended to reach older people whose opinions were tempered by fear of children, especially those whose leisure included more physical and less localised play activities.

An example of a professional working with children in neighbourhoods.
© www.johnbirdsall.co.uk

- In addition to this, the local community, whose representatives were almost without exception elderly, had a nostalgic and protective perception of their environment and wanted to replace what they believed to be the landscapes of the past, based on formal, defined play areas.
- Adult perceptions of children's so-called needs were so often relegated to the 'soft' areas, for example, contained formal play spaces. Generally, we are far too narrow in our focus of what we expect that children can or will do, particularly in the level of their interaction with adults.

The nature of the population on estates determines issues of concern and will be informed by age and access to resources. It is important to be clear about *who* the programmes are designed to benefit. A major struggle for the project workers in the Leeds scheme was to convey to the elders how children's and young people's activities have changed and therefore why facilities need to change too. Perhaps Jenks is right when he argues that, as a society, we no longer know what children are, so we cannot articulate or understand their needs (Jenks, 1996). But these attitudes to children and youth can only have a negative impact, and social development and regeneration build on notions of personal empowerment. How can these tensions be resolved?

A model of children's participation in urban regeneration

So far we have considered the dimensions of regeneration: the different roles for the involvement of the community in regeneration and the purposes of networking. But it is not easy to apply them to an evaluation of the participation of children in regeneration in a meaningful way. To take this forward, we present the following concepts as a model and consider them in the overall context of the framework outlined above.

Figure 4: A hierarchy of children's participation in regeneration

- Consultation, democracy, partnership and rights
- Consultation, democracy and partnership
- Consultation and democracy
- Consultation

Consultation

Consulting with children for regeneration projects involves asking for their opinions and sharing ideas. But that is all. There is no acknowledgement that children's voices will carry weight. Research carried out on behalf of Leeds City Council indicated a set of wide-ranging issues of concern to young people in the inner city and it stressed how they want to be consulted and involved in those issues that are important to them. Fifty-four per cent of young people surveyed wanted to tell decision makers what they thought and 50% felt that they could do something to improve their area (Leeds City Council, 1996). But in the consultation process associated with regeneration, children are too often not seen as citizens. At best they are seen as semi-citizens, and this reinforces their sense of being excluded from society.

Consultation and democracy

The process of consultation carries more credibility if it is presented as a democratic alternative to imposition. Here consultation is presumed to carry with it associations of open and fair procedures for making choices. Many young people are concerned about their future prospects and feel strongly that they have no voice. They are not listened to. A substantial minority become disaffected. Children participating in the Scottish case study were from a Priority Partnership Area (PPA) which promises a strategic and focused approach to social and economic regeneration and a commitment to broad community involvement in the regeneration process. The key issues cited by these children included the physical condition of the area (general decay, empty shops, litter and neglect), and lack of security (gangs of youths, drink and drug abuse) and these assumed primacy above lack of facilities and personal boredom. The children summarised the benefits of consultation with democracy:

- when young people and adults mix, it leads to a better atmosphere and less chance of disruption;
- young people have a part to play as members of their community;
- young people have needs but also responsibilities: too often this aspect is forgotten;
- young people need the support of sympathetic adults;
- young people need advice and information in a way that they can understand;
- an investment in young people as future citizens would benefit the whole community.

An example of successful collaborative work on consultation and democracy is in the inner-city area of Birmingham where Mercian Housing Association has consulted local schoolchildren and invited them to share in decision making about the refurbishment of local properties, where many of them live. By involving children in a democratic process, issues around both child safety and nuisance were significantly diminished, and the regeneration activity, seen to be owned by the local children, had a positive impact on the economic and social life of the area. While the public relations benefits of such an initiative should not be ignored, this was innovative activity for a housing association. The comments of one of the association's officers indicates how it had grasped an understanding of the potential future impact of seriously alienated young people: "at the end of the day the kids are a major part of the area: a bouncy castle or a clown does not engage them in the planning process.... It's hard work, but it makes you think about how you communicate, and get an understanding from their perspective". This housing association's commitment acted as a focus of stability, a clear example of the development of social capital.

Consultation, democracy and partnership

Children's participation is more plausible and meaningful if the democratic processes of consultation are combined with a real intention to forge partnerships between involved and interested groups. Children's voices are validated if they are heard on an equal footing. To illustrate how consultation, democracy and partnership might be developed, we give as an example the issues emerging from a 'standard' inner-city SRB programme developed and delivered in Leeds.

The city stands to benefit from an overall £24m regeneration programme to offer opportunities for young people between the ages of 9 and 25 in jobs, housing, education, health, recreation, the arts and environmental action. Young people were consulted during the preparation of the bid by the local authority at a series of community meetings held across the target area. However, the issues being discussed here reflect on the particular difficulties associated with drawing children into the most common consultation processes and partnerships that are associated with the more traditional aspects of urban regeneration. Why? Because consultation took place through formal committee meetings and tenants' associations structures via a local forum. The nature of the organisation to facilitate the community consultation mechanism sharply highlighted the difficulties of achieving effective participation by the very group who are seen to be part of the problem! The overwhelming feeling of residents on the estate was that young people (rather than small children) were the cause of crime. There were two places on the forum for young people but it was very difficult to get them filled. Children and young people expressed concern to project workers that they would face hostility if they joined the forum.

Spending decisions needed to be made quickly so practical measures relied on a pragmatic approach. Where the development of leisure facilities was involved, issues of age and gender were crucial. Play spaces for the under-7s proved uncontentious, but for the over-7s the focus was very much on boys. Boys were seen as the problem, and the needs of the girls' very different play patterns went unheeded. However, the young people themselves had very little impact in determining the future of leisure provision, even though they were the targets of this facility.

The issues that professionals in urban regeneration need to pay attention to when planning consultation mechanisms which are based on democracy and partnership are as follows:

- **The process:** how do we involve children in what are predominantly adult structures? Regeneration involves liaison with statutory bodies and it is difficult to access very young children because of the difficulties associated with designing 'child'-appropriate participative structures.
- **Consultation:** balancing children's and young people's issues against adult issues: who exactly are regeneration resources being invested for if not tomorrow's citizens?
- **Democracy:** how can children be empowered to develop their own alternative structures for participation?
- **Working in partnership:** seeing the benefits. Planning for Real and other participation schemes show that young people have a freshness, enthusiasm and liveliness which needs to be tapped and followed through or it will be lost

Whether or not children and adults should be separated in the decision-making process, both need to learn to cooperate with each other.

Members of community groups as well as professionals need to develop awareness of how adults and children interact. If the idea of empowerment as the key to democracy is to mean anything in the context of children and young people, it will be necessary to take some risks: for example, giving children their own budget, allowing them to make mistakes and learn from them.

Consultation, democracy, partnership and rights

True commitment to involving children in regeneration should confer rights upon them: the basic right to be consulted, the right to participate in a democratic process, the right to be viewed as partners in initiatives which inevitably impact on children's lives. There are all too few examples of this, but we examine one approach which appears to encompass all four concepts.

The Grimethorpe Initiative in South Yorkshire involves the participation of children in part of the regeneration of a former mining community experiencing high levels of unemployment and other manifestations of social exclusion. The location for the popular but poignant film *Brassed Off*, Grimethorpe is now an area of activity for a number of agencies including housing associations, one of which is Yorkshire Metropolitan Housing Association. This organisation, adopting an holistic approach to the process of regeneration, moved away from the narrow remit of the provision and management of housing and appointed a youth worker. This temporary appointment marked a significant departure for the housing association and reflected the acceptance of a multiagency, partnership approach. The main focus of the practitioner's work was to develop and implement a 'citizens' jury' for children. The housing association had become familiar with this process and its application among adults and wanted to translate it into operating with young people. With practical and financial support from Save the Children, the project was researched and firm proposals drew funding from a range of participants in the Grimethorpe Partnership.

The partnership agreed that whatever recommendations came out of the young people's jury they would be closely scrutinised and the young people would be given a speedy response as to whether or not the proposals would be accepted as viable. A process for implementation was therefore built into the structure of the project.

The process of consultation identified four major areas of concern among the young people in the area:
- the need for more and better facilities for young people;
- the need to get more children involved in community regeneration;
- the need to reduce rates of crime and drug abuse;
- the need to improve the appearance of the area.

Although there was lively debate about the possible provision of a swimming pool or rave place, by far and way the most overwhelming concern was crime and drugs. The children's responses echo those articulated in the Scottish case study and further reflect the inaccuracy of the stereotypes of young people in regeneration areas. Summaries of the evidence given by each witness to the Grimethorpe Jury were produced, and other schoolchildren were trained to write websites. A website is now up and running. The jury's findings were then presented to the Grimethorpe Partnership and the Regeneration Board.

Questions can be raised about the validity of courts, whether they enable children to give their views honestly. It is important not to give children and young people the idea that their opinions and feelings will carry more weight than they will, but the jury is a good introduction to the decision-making process. The benefits at Grimethorpe have been to enhance the combination of consultation, democracy, partnerships and rights. That children have rights has been explicitly acknowledged and a number of projects have emerged as a direct result of the partnership with the local children. These include:
- peer education on leaving home: this is a project funded jointly with Centrepoint, a homeless charity;
- Grimethorpe Partnership housing strategy;
- initiatives to improve the relationship between young people and the police.

People leading community-based urban regeneration schemes should ensure that barriers to participation are minimised. Five strategies to achieve these goals have been identified:
- Take *positive* steps to widen access (don't underestimate the capacities of any section of the community).
- Give those involved the opportunity to discuss and shape the overall process in which they will be engaged.

- Groupwork skills: the process should let everyone be heard with respect and decisions reached through consensus-seeking (empowerment of all groups).
- Agencies should be open to the outcomes of the networking process which they have stimulated (don't consult without intending to account for the results of the consultation).
- The capacity to link networks and develop forums and 'clearing-houses for experience' is a valuable resource (structures for children may need to be different) (Skelcher et al, 1996).

These guidelines appear to reflect the reality of the Grimethorpe activity and, if implemented coherently, should allow for consultation, democracy, partnership and rights for the children who are living through the delivery of urban regeneration.

Concluding comments

Children are resident in communities or neighbourhoods in the same sense as adults. However, they are rarely invited to participate in the decision-making processes concerning potentially far-reaching changes to the extent that adults are. Yet children can bring with them a range of often unconsidered benefits including a reduction in general tensions, usually involving the use of public/play space. More importantly, involving children can lead to the development of future participative communities and, ultimately, the development of social sustainability (West, 1998).

Children must be seen as stakeholders in area regeneration and as vital to the concept of capacity building. Their participation in activities associated with regeneration therefore has a role on the wider agenda of lifelong learning and the development of citizenship skills (Henderson and Mayo, 1998). Children, however, have been subject to a considerable amount of negative stereotyping, and this is nowhere more apparent than in the context of urban regeneration where so much of the focus has been on deprivation, disadvantage and social exclusion. But the voices of children themselves tell us that they share our concerns for their neighbourhoods and for the future of their communities. It is the responsibility of those professionals involved in the delivery of urban regeneration to ensure that children are involved in the process, that they are consulted, that they are involved in a democratic process, that they are accepted as part of the partnership and that their rights are acknowledged.

EIGHT

Children's physical environment

Introduction

In Colin Ward's *The child in the city* the riveting black and white photographs give a message that children are ever-present in urban neighbourhoods. The cover shows children playing by a canal, as one lone adult looks on somewhat warily. The author makes the following plea:

> We have enormous expertise and a mountain of research on the appropriate provision of parks and play spaces.... Because some bit of the city is designated as a play space on a plan, there is no guarantee that it will be used as such, nor that other areas will not be. If the claim of children to share the city is to be admitted, the whole environment has to be designed and shaped with their needs in mind.... (Ward, 1978, p 204)

It is doubtful if the photographs that bring Ward's 1978 edition to life could have been re-taken for the edition of his book in 1990 which comes as pure text. What has happened in the interim? Why is it no longer common to see large groups of unaccompanied children by the canal? Canals still exist and if anything are far cleaner and more scenic in the 1990s than in the 1970s, but they are no longer seen as legitimate places for unaccompanied children to be. Now, police making their school visits warn children to stay away from canals and also not to cross roads without an adult. The outdoor environment is portrayed as out of bounds and unsafe.

It would be wrong to view the 1970s as some halcyon age for children, but children's environmental rights are being eroded. Why is this and does it matter? What constitutes a good environment for the child, what does it look like, what are its components, how can it be used, and where should it be? Some people would say there is a prior question: does children's physical environment actually matter?

Debates concerning the extent to which environment influences children's behaviours are not new. The nature–nurture debate poses the question of which has the greater influence – genetic inheritance or upbringing? Similarly, the social construction of gender debate asks whether the behavioural differences between boys and girls are due primarily to innate genetic differences or to differences in upbringing and gendered societal influences. A similar debate can be held regarding the relative influence of the physical environment as opposed to the social and cultural environment in children's development. As with the two earlier debates there is no unequivocal answer, but reason suggests that both physical and socio-cultural environments will influence children's lives and development opportunities.

This chapter examines the range of children's physical environments. It asks, how does society influence children's use of the environment and what sort of environment do children themselves want? We do not make the case for an ideal environment. Environments are not static; they are continually evolving and they incorporate and reflect the full extent of societal diversity. Indeed it is this diversity that gives our environments much of their appeal. What this chapter does do is identify some key issues for consideration by professionals whose actions shape the environments in which children live.

Children's environmental needs and wants

Yet children's concerns are rarely considered by professions which have environmental responsibilities: what children think about their environment and how they experience that environment. Consideration of 'marginalised' groups such as women, disabled people, members of minority ethnic groups and elderly people is increasing and certainly is incorporated into professional training programmes such as those undertaken by planners. By way of contrast, little if any consideration is given to children as a special group with specific environmental views and requirements. This is especially disquieting when those professions whose actions directly influence children's environmental experience – planners, housing officers, architects, environmental health officers, engineers and landscape architects – ignore children. Accordingly, it is not surprising that the environment-focused professions, especially those dealing with the regulation and design of the built environment, are ill-equipped to consider or meet children's needs.

Within the environmental/land-use management professions there is no articulation of children's needs as they relate to the totality of their environment. There are design and building standards for specific children's spaces such as playgrounds and schools. This would be fine if children lived all their lives in schools and playgrounds, but they don't. They live in houses. They shop, travel, and in some cases work in the same environment as their adult counterparts. The fundamental issue is, as Ward points out, "to make the whole environment child friendly".

When they are given opportunities to articulate a clear set of environmental concerns, many of children's likes and dislikes are not dissimilar to those articulated by adults. Aspects of their environment identified by children in the consultation carried out for this report included litter, vandalism, graffiti, street gangs, empty shops, run-down appearance, general neglect, too many cars, pot holes in the road, not enough buses, lack of security, lack of facilities and pollution from factories and acid rain. Conversely, things identified as good included a peaceful atmosphere, trees and gardens, views of the castle (Dunbarton), clean environment, countryside, safe environments and public transport (despite its inadequacies). Environmental concerns clearly rated highly on the children's agendas.

The negative and positive aspects identified by children would not be significantly different to those identified by adults. One vital but seldom acknowledged truth is that an environment that is better for children is one that is also better for adults, especially those with special needs such as disabled and elderly people, and those with caring responsibilities. Exploration of the developing literature on disability perhaps most clearly demonstrates this. In his exploration of disability, Gleeson identifies physical representations of discrimination which can take a number of forms:

- Physical barriers to movement including, for example, broken surfaces and slippery pavements.
- Building architecture which excludes the entry of anyone unable to use stairs and open handed doors impacts on wheelchair users, those with a shopping trolley, or those carrying shopping in both hands. Turnstiles present particular problems for many adults though not for children who can squeeze through or under them.
- Public and private transport modes which assume that driver and passengers are non-impaired (eg carers with small children, visually impaired, pregnant women, small people and children who can't see over the ticket counters or reach speaking phones or the holes in the glass to speak through to order their ticket, short people who cannot

reach the 'hold on' handles that dangle from the roof – most regular bus travellers can relate experiences of being 'fallen on' by standing passengers failing to hang on as buses negotiate turns).

- Public information (eg signage) presented in forms that assume a common level of visual and aural ability (Gleeson, 1999).

All the above reduce children's accessibility to the urban environment but there can be few adults who have not also grappled with the above, even if it is just through falling on a slippery, ill-designed wet pavement surface. There are also few adults who will not at some time in their lives require a more accessible environment either for themselves or through their caring responsibilities.

The development of environments that benefit everyone has been the focus of recently released urban design guides such as *The Essex design guide for residential and mixed use areas* (Essex County Council, 1998). As with the disability example discussed above, the design recommendations that characterise these guides offer benefits to all sectors of the community, especially children, through the provision of safe, accessible, diverse neighbourhoods which emphasise small-scale local spaces and which are pedestrian friendly.

While well-designed environments benefit all in society, the impact of negative factors such as cars, vandalism, street gangs and safety are often more apparent for children than for adults. The perceived lack of safety has forced many children back into their homes and away from public space. It has meant that children are rarely free of adult supervision, as Mayer Hillman's well-known survey of the declining mobility of school-aged children between 1971 and 1990 demonstrates (Hillman, 1993). Vandalism, which is greatly disliked by the community as a whole, is particularly prevalent in parks and play areas, often resulting in children being unable to use equipment such as swings and roundabouts. For many children the constraints and the effects of environmental disrepair affect the quality of their daily lives. Urban form and qualities are, however, not constant. Environments can change and, as indicated in Chapter 7, this is where regeneration programmes have the potential to make a significant positive impact on neighbourhoods.

Changing environments

In his description of his childhood in Leeds, Steven Owen observes that:

As a small boy in the 1950s I went to Leeds almost every week [by bus]. It was a grim experience ... looking down into Leeds revealed only a heavy, greyish-brown pall through which few buildings were visible and through which little sunlight ever penetrated except during bank holidays when the factories were idle ... most of the buildings were black; even the river was black streaked with iridescent oil. The air was gritty; there were no trees.... It was inconceivable that towns might be enjoyable places. (Owen, 1991, p ix)

It is a description that contrasts vividly with the Leeds of today which is experiencing substantial regeneration. Physical environments, whether they are urban or rural, are in a continuous state of change. It is change that reflects the social and economic imperatives of the day but it is change that can also be directly related to the beliefs and actions of the land-use professions. Thus, responsibility for the deprivation currently experienced by children condemned to live in tower blocks and on run-down housing estates lies in part with politicians and in part with architects, builders, engineers, planners, housing professionals and others who were involved in creating the living areas. Undoubtedly lessons have been learnt from this experiment in 'housing design', but for many children these lessons come too late. Physical change is accompanied by community changes. When tracing the changes in the environment and their impact on children's lives two distinct but irrevocably linked strands have to be assessed: changes in urban form and changes in the social environment.

Changes in urban form

Two key, connected changes in urban form have been the regeneration and restoration initiatives that have transformed many cities, especially city centres, and changes associated with the growth in traffic. In general the latter has contributed to the decentralisation of industry, shops and services away from the centres and an associated decline in public transport services. This has then impacted specifically on key public amenities such as health centres and shopping centres. Decentralisation processes that particularly affect children include the trend towards closing local cinemas and swimming pools while opening large cinema and leisure complexes which are increasingly located at motorway junctions or on peripheral retail sites which can only be reached by car.

Traffic growth significantly impacts on children's lives and, with the relentless growth in traffic volume, the situation facing children worsens:

- Erosion of children's independent mobility, with related effects on emotional and social development.
- Health impacts through pollution and loss of fitness.
- Road accidents: 100,000 children were victims of traffic accidents between 1983 and 1993 (Hillman, 1993). Overall, road accident levels in Britain are decreasing. However, such statistics have to be treated with caution. Some of the reduction is because fewer people, especially children, are on the street. While cars are becoming safer for their passengers, the victims of accidents are increasingly likely to be pedestrians, cyclists or other 'unprotected' road users.
- Increased escorting of children by parents and carers.
- Costs of traffic congestion due in part to increased chauffeuring of children.
- Loss of social opportunities as fewer people use streets and local facilities so that children have fewer opportunities to observe adults going about their lives outside the home.

There are two ways of dealing with the growing impact of transport on children's lives: to continue to withdraw children from the growing threat or to address the threat through traffic reduction schemes whereby neighbourhoods are reclaimed from the car. In Holland, traffic-calming methods such as the use of ramps have been combined with the creation of 'home zones' where children's play is given more importance than cars. Drivers know that if they hit a child they will be held legally responsible. The effect has been to persuade drivers to take more care and to drive more slowly. The UK government is supporting nine pilot projects. A number of residents' groups have introduced their own schemes.

While recognising the negative impacts of increasing car use and the greater degree of escorting, for many children there are also associated benefits. These include more opportunities for undertaking activities, experiences presented by the greater access that cars provide and the social benefits provided to both children and their parents through increased involvement in children's lives through escorting. Overall, however, children's rights to safety in the neighbourhood should be paramount and this necessities concerted traffic reduction and safety campaigns.

A related issue and one that is being addressed by an increasing range of professions is that of play. The Charter for Children's Play, developed by the National Voluntary Council for Children's Play, states:

All neighbourhoods should have a range of play provision and play services. Children should be able to play safely near their homes with friends ... children's provision should be planned with community involvement. Architects, planners and builders should work together with statutory, voluntary and private play services managers and workers, community and parents groups children and other relevant parties.... (National Voluntary Council for Children's Play, 1994, p 11)

As children's play range has decreased due largely to growing parental fears for their children's safety, the neighbourhood environment has become increasingly important for play. Millward and Wheway, in their survey of play on housing estates, found that it was "the outdoor environment within two streets of the front door" that was the most important location for neighbourhood play. The most successful estates for play were found to be those with:

- traffic calming, street closure, walls and driveways;
- grassy areas set back from roads, a footpath network linking into open spaces;
- cul-de-sacs with spinal footpath network, and informal play areas.

The researchers also note, however, the extent to which 'purposeful movement' is important for children:

This finding is crucial to an understanding of how children use their environment and why designing housing estates to facilitate pedestrian and cycle movement for children is so important. Interviews with children revealed very definite ideas on preferred play places. What is clear is that they travel from one to another, trying them out and meeting different friends. (Millard and Wheway, 1997, p 4)

While design is important it is essential that children be given places both to experience and to manipulate the environment, putting their own creative stamp on it through building dens, rope swings, skateboard and bmx obstacles, digging and rearranging it (a process usually disparagingly referred to as making a mess). A manicured, formal environment precludes such activities. Informal natural environments are as important as equipped play parks in meeting children's play needs. They enable children to acquire and value a sense of place identity:

> The process of attachment can go on for years with a layering of successive play episodes. And the result of this intensity of experience of place will be reflected in a sense of being strong enough to use 'placeness' and rootedness to describe the feeling of affiliation. (Adams, 1995, p 159)

Children are the greatest users of the local outdoor environment and again the premise applies that an enriched and safe environment for children has benefits for everyone. However, it is not only physical change that has affected children's lives and their environmental access, but parallel processes of social change.

Social changes

"Childhood is a reflection of prevailing societal attitudes and priorities providing an interpretive framework for contextualising the early years … [it] is neither a natural nor a universal feature of human groups but appears as a specific structural and cultural component of many societies" (James and Prout, 1990, p 8). Childhood cannot be separated from other variables of social analysis such as class, gender or ethnicity. How is this social construction reflected in and influenced by the physical form of the environment in which children lead their lives? Some of the physical variables such as growing car use have already been alluded to, but as soon as social factors are introduced the issue becomes more complex.

One characteristic of children's social lives in Britain has been that they are becoming more controlled and more separate from adults' lives. This twin-track process has been referred to as the increasing 'governance' of children. The perceived risk of children as threats has led to suggestions by both members of the public and government that children should be subject to curfews and greater behavioural control. Conversely, the perceived risk of children as victims has led to greater involvement of children in adult supervised activities, and the growth in what has been termed the 'domestification' of play. This is where children are encouraged, even forced, to play indoors under supervision. This phenomenon feeds the expansion of consumerism because it supports the purchase of toys, computer games and other more sedentary, 'safe' activities which can be undertaken within the supervised home environment. The pressure to buy children's consumer goods has the effect, in time, of keeping children in the private domain of the home.

Is the general perception of the 'outside' environment as being increasingly hostile valid? There is no statistical evidence to support the perception that the environment is becoming more dangerous. However, perceptions of danger are not usually based on statistics but on people's perceptions, often strongly influenced by the media. It is useful for planners and others to categorise the different degrees of seriousness of danger, perhaps using a continuum to do this – from uneven pavements to the housing of sex offenders (see Table 7). More clear-cut than perceptions of danger is the trend towards decreased tolerance of perceived anti-social behaviour, physical violence and potentially dangerous situations such as dangers posed by high slides or uneven pavements. For the most part, the message of low or zero tolerance, as in high-profile anti-bullying campaigns and campaigns by groups such as ChildLine against child abuse, are positive. However, care must be taken to ensure that there is room for expressions of 'difference' and opportunities for children and young people to express themselves in public. They need to have legitimate and safe opportunities to socialise with their peers and with wider society. At present, these opportunities are not present. The social needs of children are not being supported by the physical environment. The next section assesses what constitutes a child-friendly environment and how such an environment might be achieved.

Children's environmental needs

There is no universal definition of children's environmental rights in the way that there are accepted understandings of, for example, children's rights in relation to work, sexual exploitation, education and health. In many cases the effects of the environment can be addressed but there is no requirement to address the causes of the problems – poor, overcrowded housing and inadequate play facilities that often contribute to the tensions that lead to family violence. There are no standards governing children's rights in the built environment. For example, there is no requirement to provide child-sized toilets, for doors to have handles at a suitable height and which are not too heavy to be opened by children, for children to be housed at ground-floor level in multi-storey housing. In all these cases, building regulations are increasingly addressing the issue of provision for disabled people but not, as yet, for children.

Table 7: Degrees of danger and levels of concern

Danger type	Frequency	Degree of damage/ harm	Level of concern – for most of population	Groups with particular concerns
Uneven surfaces	Common	Usually low	Low	Young children, those with impaired mobility
Accidents from playground equipment	Low to mixed	Usually low (especially with move to safety surfaces)	Low	Children
Obstacles to movement eg shop goods on street	Common	Nuisance rather than danger	Low	Visually impaired
Health problems associated with poor housing	Common for lower socio-economic groups	Long-term effects	Mixed	Children and elderly
Bullying	Common	Varies	Low but growing	Children, women, elderly
Drugs including alcohol and cigarettes	Common	Can be severe	Mixed but growing	Teenagers and parents (drugs), families (alcohol)
Mugging and street violence	Varies	Mixed, can be severe	Low	Young men. High in some circumstances eg after dark for women
Violence in the home	Unknown, suspected to be common	Can be severe and long term	Mixed, growing concern	Children, women, elderly
Traffic accidents	Common	Often severe	High	Children pedestrians
Attack/abduction from strangers	Rare	Severe	Very high	Children
Sex offenders	Rare	Severe	Very high	Children

The main reason why the question of children's environmental rights is not tackled by politicians and decision makers is to do with resources: to address such rights would have significant financial consequences. Who, for example, would provide the resources necessary to ensure that all children have adequate and uncrowded housing? And who would take responsibility for creating car-free safe play neighbourhoods? While it is not realistic to change all environments so that they are, if not child-friendly, at least not child-alienating, it is possible to try and bring children's needs forward and include them in the ongoing process of environmental change and development. Pressure must therefore be put on politicians and decision makers by a range of adult and children's organisations. That is the only way of challenging the resources argument.

In evaluating and planning for the environment it is essential to remember the extent to which children's environmental experiences differ from those of adults, for only then can child-friendly environments be supported. In their research examining children's relationships with both their physical and social environment, Matthews and Limb argue that, until recognition is given to the different ways adults and children experience the environment, children will remain marginalised within society. The distinctions between children and adults that they identify include:

- Assumptions are made about what it means to be a child and therefore what environments children need. In so doing there is a failure to recognise that children differ from adults in terms of their 'ways of seeing'. What goes on during the day of an average child is different in rhythm, scale and content from that of adults.
- Land uses and facilities which involve children are frequently different from those of adults and even when shared are largely used for different purposes (eg adults use parks for a quiet stroll or sit on the bench, children for a game of football).
- Free access of children, and the types of environmental setting they can enter, are often more restricted (note the proliferation of 'no unaccompanied children' notices in corner shops).
- Children often encounter threats in the environment that go unnoticed by adults.
- Children's interpretation and evaluation of places will differ from that of adults. Their views on environmental planning are unlikely to coincide.
- Children are unable to influence decision making and processes which determine the structure of environments in general and land uses in particular.

- Involving children in the design and management of their environment is a valued end in itself, as well as an important step towards developing competent, participating citizens (Matthews and Limb, 1999).

To provide good environments for children it is necessary to identify those elements that constitute a good environment. The following represents a list of children's environmental rights which would contribute to child-friendly environments. They should be considered in the context of the underlying principle determining environmental design for a child-friendly environment: to achieve greater equity between the needs of adults and children.

The first stage in creating child-friendly environments must be for professionals to acknowledge the legitimacy of children's environmental rights, including their right (and the right of their carers) to participate in determining environmental use and design. The following represent other key environmental rights:

- access to the whole city or countryside environment;
- being part of the community;
- having access to the natural environment;
- being able to use and reasonably access public services;
- physical environments and public services that recognise children's specific needs;
- designing public spaces which take into account children's needs;
- being able to move about freely;
- being able to travel safely;
- having areas designed specifically to meet children's needs.

When addressing children's physical environmental needs, professionals may find that they are entering unfamiliar territory. There is little guidance on children's environmental rights, in contrast to health and educational rights. If the principles identified in this book, such as the right to be consulted, the right to participate in decision making, the right to high quality environments, are met, the form that the environment takes is important. Children are flexible and adaptable, and there is no one 'right' environment. As a baseline, if, as Ward requests, children's right to the whole environment is acknowledged, then progress is being made. The environments that children experience determine not only their health, social and economic opportunities but also their environmental perceptions and attitudes. Thus the provision of a healthy, challenging and safe environment is, for professionals, a long-term investment in the future.

Planning and children: Lismore, New South Wales, Australia

The aim of the project undertaken by Cunningam et al (1996) was to give some insight into children's use of the environment, specifically, how children in middle childhood (8- to 12-year-olds) used their after-school leisure time for independent play. One of the issues to be addressed was the influence of the car and television on children's play patterns. Lismore is a rural provincial city with a sub-tropical climate with the usual low density housing associated with Australian towns and cities. A range of methods were used to gain a picture of children's play patterns including surveys of parents, children at school, households and observation studies of the neighbourhood. However, the most important method used was a photographic study by children themselves. Twenty-four children from three schools were given disposable cameras and asked to take photographs while they played after school; 342 usable photos resulted.

The location of the images taken was as follows, with no noticeable difference between boys and girls: home and back yard 53%, street near home 6%, parks 17% and open or natural areas 24%, showing the importance attributed to immediate home environment. Children in Goonellabah, which is a newer more motor-oriented suburb, appear to have more restricted play ranges than children in the older established suburbs. The images that appear in the photos were as follows: home building itself 10%, formal play areas at home 24%, naturalistic areas 41%, street and street objects 4%, formal play areas 21%. A higher propensity to photograph naturalistic settings was noted in Goonellabah where such settings were more accessible. The number of images by sex showed the importance of mixed gender play (the statistics underestimate the degree of mixing as often the photographer was a different gender to those being photographed: only boys 41%, mixed gender 20%, only girls 35%, adults present 4%. The study ends with the following words from the children of Goonellabah School:

Ashley, Casey, Brian and Brett from Goonellabah public school would like the town planners to understand the needs of children and where they like to play ... we think it is a good idea if planners look at photos taken by kids of their favourite places and then maybe when they are drawing up the town or the city they should put more parks in and leave scrub areas where they are. (Cunningham et al, 1996)

The method used in the project summarised above was similar to one used in the Patio Project in Rotherham, South Yorkshire and described here by one of the practitioners:

"I asked a group of children to show me places on the estate which were important to where they live, play etc. I handed over the project's camera and encouraged them to take photos of anything that interested them."

"I began with a group of four children but as we walked around the estate the group grew to over ten, all wanting to take photos. Each part of the estate had significance to some or all of the children and they told me about this as we went along: 'we're not supposed to go down there'; 'we play outside the shop'; 'we have a lot of empty houses and a lot of rubbish.'"

"I repeated this process three times, always allowing the children to lead the way and take the photos. What I had learnt was that they had strong views and opinions about their neighbourhood and also that they experienced it and used it in a very different way to older children and adults: a burnt-out dustbin store being a den one day, a hiding place the next but never what it was – a burnt-out dustbin store that looked a mess. Children's experience differs so much from adults; they have the ability to create something interesting and exciting from nothing!'" (Wood, 1998, p 2)

One of the children involved with the Patio Project (now known as Rotherham Participation Project) takes a photograph of part of the estate.
© The Children's Society

NINE

Planning with children

Children and young people – hopes for the future? © Ed Freeman

In the preceding chapters we have made the case for children's participation at neighbourhood level and in relevant decision-making processes. In this final chapter we draw together the core themes and focus on the question of how children's participation can become an accepted and integral part of the professional practice of planners, architects, housing officers, regeneration staff and other professionals. What are the conditions which will enable this to happen? How can professionals – managers as well as practitioners – act so that children play a direct role in determining the environment and life of neighbourhoods?

The chapter will move from the abstract to the specific. We begin by revisiting the key conceptual 'territory' which informs planning with children for better communities. Then we discuss a number of 'middle range' strategic questions and key practice points. Finally, we put forward a policy and practice framework for planning with children, linking action at local, regional and national levels.

Key ideas

It is mistaken for practitioners and managers to think that they can develop participative approaches to working with children in isolation from theory development and research findings on children and society. They need to be aware of key ideas because these will influence their own thinking and action. This is doubly important in the field of children's participation because of the extent to which it draws upon several academic disciplines such as sociology, psychology, social policy and environmental planning. Each discipline is researching and writing about particular aspects of children's lives. From time to time, evidence and findings from more than one discipline appear to coalesce, providing new insights and guidance.

At the same time, theory and research can, implicitly or explicitly, provide a challenge to everyday assumptions. The research carried out by the European Centre for Social Welfare Policy and Research was an example of this because, by placing children as the central unit of observation, it demonstrated how children can speak and act for themselves (Qvortrup, 1991). The paper by Moss and Petrie provides a similar kind of theoretical challenge in the policy sphere. By seeking to understand the 'dominant discourse' on the relationship between children, parents and society, it is able to put forward an alternative discourse in the context of children's services, based on "a coherent and holistic policy towards childhood and children, a recognised place for children in society as well as in the family, and respect for children and the promotion of their rights" (Moss and Petrie, 1997, p 3). The authors point out that the dominant discourse is strongly individualistic and, if this perspective is valid, it clearly has implications for professionals who are seeking to support children's participation. They contend that change is needed in how we think about children, parents and society, and they argue for "an alternative ideological and intellectual framework."

The Economic and Social Research Council's research programme *Children 5-16: Growing into the Twenty-First Century* (1997-2000) may result in the strengthening of such a framework. The programme is multidisciplinary and aims to make a significant contribution to our knowledge of the changing conditions of childhood and children's everyday lives as well as theoretical and methodological advances in the study of children as social actors. It is certainly the kind of academic work with which practitioners and managers need to keep in touch, not simply because it will be of interest but because the findings and outcomes will permeate and shape thinking and policy development.

There is little that is as powerful as a good idea. We have seen in earlier chapters the influence on planners of Arnstein's ladder of participation. Another example, this time in the community development field, has been the writing of Sandra Schoenberg, who put forward the following propositions regarding what makes a viable neighbourhood:

- agreements about public order and ways of dealing with breaches of agreements;
- existence of lasting organisations in neighbourhoods;
- linkages to resources;
- exchange between people – the ability of groups to 'give and take' and to deal with conflicts (Schoenberg, 1979).

It is worth reflecting on the extent to which these four propositions have influenced the thinking of both policy makers and practitioners, not necessarily in ways that can be directly attributed to Schoenberg, but as part of the climate or process of discussing and clarifying ideas about neighbourhoods prior to or as part of an intervention programme. Certainly we can see them echoed in the government's policy papers on regeneration and social inclusion. We can also see their influence on organisations which have based resources and services in neighbourhoods: the necessity of supporting and building community organisations which last, and the need to have informal 'rules' about how different members of a community – children, young people, elderly people – manage to live alongside each other.

The issue of children's participation is, inescapably, part of public debate and it surfaces in a variety of contexts. In 1999, for example, the Mental Health Foundation published the findings of an inquiry into the mental health of children and young people. The interesting feature of the report is the extent to which, alongside specialist sections, it addresses many questions raised in this book, particularly those surrounding the issue of risk and the effect on children of their lack of freedom to play unsupervised:

> Unsupervised play enables children to take risks, to think through decisions and gain increased self-confidence and greater resilience. However, as a result of parental fears, and the seeming priority given to cars over the need of children, many children's ability to play has been severely curtailed. (Mental Health Foundation, 1999, p 36)

Thus many of the key ideas which either underpin or which inform children's participation are generic and they enter into a range of professional worlds – the example given above relates to social work but the same themes of exclusion, discrimination and risk are relevant to planners, housing officers, play workers and many others. This phenomenon, and the challenges it presents to professionals, underlies the need for them to keep returning to the key ideas, to engage with them rather than – consciously or unconsciously – seeing them as distant to their concerns. It is because fundamental questions about children and society have been neglected that "we have not developed services, policies and government structures that adequately recognise and meet the needs and interests of children as a social group" (Moss and Petrie, 1997, p 16).

Strategic and practice issues

Being clear about working principles for planning with children must be a priority for all professional groups. We have discussed earlier the importance of acting in partnership with other organisations and the need to tackle the issue of obtaining permissions from parents and other adults. Questions surrounding the protection of children and dangers of child abuse are so close to the surface in any community that, to put it mildly, it would be naïve or irresponsible – or both – not to address them. The amount of time needed to do this should not be underestimated.

It is also essential that professionals think through how they propose to go about their work. If possible, this should be done in a team situation and the objective should be for practitioners and managers to be clear as to what is agreed, communicating this to other organisations as appropriate. We are not suggesting that there is a blueprint for the kind of checklist being suggested because it is important that points made are 'owned' by those involved. The following list of indicators of good practice provides a good model. They were drawn up by a group of workers in the Glasgow Child Poverty Project:

- Acknowledge the power difference between children and adults. Failure to do so can lead to manipulation
- Recognise that childhood is both related to and separate from the adult world
- Establish a balance between process and product
- Understand that what children have to say may not be the same as what adults want to hear

- Create space to enable children to say what they mean
- Involve children in formulating the questions. If possible involve them in asking the questions
- Provide a supportive adult context – staff of carers who are sympathetic to a participative approach
- Note that children's and adults' conceptions of time may vary. Usually this means that children like to have quick feedback from what they have said or done.

The group also noted that good quality participative work is most likely to take place in trusted, stable groupings which last over time: after school groups, clubs, school classes etc. (Wood, 1999, p 18)

In developing good practice principles or indicators, two things become clear: the need to be very specific and the importance of turning to other professionals, particularly those who are trained to work with children, for advice and inputs. Where appropriate, specialist staff should be recruited, a point made in a study of young people in urban regeneration: "Resources and staffing are critical. There is a need for dedicated workers" (Fitzpatrick et al, 1998, p 36)

Discipline and rigour in planning for children's participation is particularly important in the neighbourhood context because of the latter's open-ended nature. In contrast, for example, to a school, it is difficult to control who gets involved and it is for that reason that a planned and structured approach is required. Adopting such an approach will lead practitioners into considering the question of which methods to use when planning work with adults, children and mixed groups which, as suggested in earlier chapters, should put a premium on informality, activities and small groups.

Policy and practice framework

It will be useful for practitioners and managers to have some reference points to which they can turn to support their work with and on behalf of children. The following is a simple framework.

Existing knowledge

The volume of publications, research reports and practice guidelines relating to planning with children for better communities is considerable and it is advisable to have a system for scanning and filtering the flow of information. It is vital, however, that professionals are aware of what is available and make a point of accessing it, especially if their own training and experience has not given them a strong knowledge base for children's participation. While most of the material cited in this book relates to the UK, we remind readers of the international context of children's rights and children's participation – many of the methods referred to earlier, such as participatory action research, have been used widely, particularly in Southern countries. The benefits to be gained from learning about initiatives in other countries can be powerful, whether this be affirming an approach already being taken or suggesting a different way of tackling a problem. Accordingly, it is worthwhile being put on mailing lists and using e-mail and the Internet to find out about experiences elsewhere. The following example of a useful resource comes from Ireland.

> **The Children's Research Centre, Trinity College Dublin** was set up in 1995. It is a multidisciplinary research centre and works in close collaboration with practitioners and policy makers. One of its key themes is children in disadvantaged communities. It notes that there has been an expansion of community and school-based projects developing new approaches to the situation of children in these communities. The centre has researched innovative approaches and techniques for responding to specific child-related issues in the community. It has also researched new community models for integrating the local provision of health, welfare and educational support services to children and young people, and it has developed methods for both planning and evaluating community-based children's projects. The centre has a strong commitment to dissemination of reports and research findings and it has its own website (http://www.tcd.ie/ Childrens_Centre/).

Within the UK, sources of information and knowledge include the local government associations, national children's organisations, local projects and research institutes. It is essential that the person or unit responsible for accessing information ensures that this is done across a number of disciplines and professions and that they are aware of relevant networks. For example, there is an Interdisciplinary Childhood and Youth Studies Network which provides a forum for developing and supporting knowledge and skills in work with children and young people (e-mail: p.t.hume@anglia.ac.uk).

Corporate approach

The case study of Durham County Council summarised in Chapter 1 is of particular interest both because its 'Investment in Children' initiative is being undertaken with other organisations and because it is situated in the centre of the authority's planning and decision-making processes. Ensuring that children's participation forms part of an agency's overall policy and strategy can be important. It means, for example, that if an approach is piloted in one area, there would be a commitment by the agency to evaluating it and considering whether or not to implement it elsewhere.

Relying only on the flair and enthusiasm of practitioners to include children in planning and regeneration processes is not good enough. We know from experience in related fields that commitment from the organisation as a whole is needed; otherwise the chances of initiatives being sustained will be slim. Furthermore, groups in the community will sometimes need to turn to managers and politicians for support – they will need people in positions of power to 'champion' a particular cause. Accordingly, making sure that there are channels of communication between fieldworkers and senior management throughout the process of a project is important.

Keeping new approaches going is a key issue in a field such as children's participation which is always susceptical to the volatility of public opinion. We have noted at different points how children's rights can be opposed by different sectors of society. Remaining firm in the face of opposition to the issue will usually require the support of several people in an organisation, if not the organisation as a whole. It will also need national and international children's organisations to maintain their commitment to children's participation and to sustain the flow of resources for research, publications, conferences and innovative projects.

Training

Committing time and resources for training practitioners on particular aspects of supporting children's participation is essential. One way of doing this is to access national and regional courses run by children's organisations, universities and others. Or a decision can be made to combine training with consultancy brought into the organisation or project on an in-house basis. This has the advantage of providing follow-up to a training experience.

The importance of having a strategic approach to training in regeneration is gaining wider recognition. It may be possible to link training on children's participation with other topics such as auditing community needs. In some parts of the country there are regional groups and networks which provide a range of training opportunities on different aspects of working with communities (Henderson and Mayo, 1998).

Evaluation

Ensuring that initiatives in the field of children's participation are evaluated is the final component of the policy and practice framework. The 10 building blocks of community development listed in Chapter 1 form the basis of an evaluation model developed by the Scottish Community Development Centre (SCDC). Devised originally as a handbook for Northern Ireland's Department of Health and Social Services (Barr et al, 1996), the approach has been disseminated through a series of training courses throughout the UK and Ireland. It is an approach which is particularly relevant to planning with children because it provides a framework which is flexible enough to be applicable at policy, programme or project level and which is sufficiently adaptable to reflect the particular priorities of community development activity at different times. It encourages communities themselves to identify indicators and information against which change can be identified, thereby encouraging practitioners and managers to involve children themselves in the evaluation process. Further information about this evaluation model can be obtained from SCDC's website (http://www.scdc.org.uk).

The importance of evaluating children's participation needs to be stressed. Children, local people, funders and others – enthusiasts and sceptics alike – need to know the outcomes of initiatives.

Concluding comments

Our concern in this book has been to bring to the attention of professionals the issue of children's participation, to encourage them to include it in their practice and to suggest approaches and methods which they can use. Hopefully, professional associations and institutes will develop a stronger commitment to the issue and both qualifying and post-qualifying training courses will include more material on it. It is, therefore, primarily a question of changing attitudes. There is no expectation of rapid change. Rather, the hope is that ideas and methods will permeate practice over time. Through exchanges and networking, people and organisations will learn from each other. Examples of practice and strategies will be evaluated and written about and – as a result of these processes – planning with children for better communities will become part of mainstream professional practice.

It would be naïve, however, to think that these processes of learning and testing out can take place in a vacuum. They will only become a reality if they take place within a positive policy climate. There are two aspects to this – mechanisms and social inclusion.

Mechanisms

In earlier chapters we highlighted the need to have mechanisms centrally and locally designed to insist that children's rights are addressed (Chapter 3), and a code of practice which monitors the extent to which children's opinions are taken into account by local authorities and other organisations (Chapter 5). We return to these at this point because it is essential that the arguments made for them by campaiging and voluntary organisations are sustained. Without them there is a danger that children's participation will be perceived to be too woolly – well-intentioned but vague – and the momentum that has gathered pace will falter.

Stronger links need to be made between professional practitioners and those organisations working for local and national mechanisms. In 1998, the Children's Rights Office of the Children's Rights Development Unit (CRDU) decided to open its membership to a range of voluntary and statutory organisations, creating an alliance committed to full implementation of the UN Convention on the Rights of the Child. It identified three interlinked objectives:

• to democratise control of CRDU;
• to make children's rights visible;
• to promote a wide range of collaborative activities.

This move by CRDU to broaden its appeal is interesting and adds weight to the argument that a new phase on implementation of the Convention is needed, one that encourages children's rights and needs to be taken up at local, neighbourhood level and one which seeks to integrate planning with children into the day-to-day practice of a range of professionals. It will be essential for this shift to be supported by children's organisations in both the voluntary and statutory sectors, professional bodies and local authorities and community organisations which are committed to involving children in their activities. Durham

County Council proposes to launch Investing in Children as a membership organisation. It is developments such as this which, taking place across the country, will add significant weight to the advocacy and campaigning work of national organisations.

Social inclusion

The social and economic context in which children's participation has been explored in this report has been of an unequal society in which the extent of child poverty, deprived neighbourhoods and excluded communities has been extensively documented. Even Treasury figures reveal that two out of every five children in the UK are born poor. The Joseph Rowntree Foundation's Inquiry into Income and Wealth states:

> We are concerned by the position of children being brought up in low-income families, particularly those in neighbourhoods where most families are poor. (Hills, 1995, p 8)

The government is tackling the issues of poverty and social exclusion as it defines them with energy and commitment. Some of its measures and proposals may arouse controversy, but its determination to make an impact on the issues cannot be questioned. In 1999 Tony Blair declared that his government wanted to provide equal opportunities for all children in 20 years (Walker, 1999).

Whether or not this ambition is realistic is not being debated here. What we wish to convey is that, at the same time that programmes and schemes are introduced to tackle child poverty, measures have to be put in place which lead both to changes in how society as a whole treats children and to changes in neighbourhoods and the agencies providing services to them. Here the intentions of the government are less clear. There is little sign that it is prepared to engage with such far-reaching ideas.

Communities which are excluded from mainstream society are where planning with children has to take place. It is here that serious efforts need to be made to engage both with children and young people – to find out from them how they are prepared to be involved – and with adults. If the idea of social inclusion is to be meaningful, community empowerment, and support for the processes which lead to empowerment, has to be a priority.

We insert, therefore, a cautionary note. *Planning with children for better communities* speaks to our more idealistic, optimistic natures. It is easy to be carried along by enthusiasm generated at a local level and by an exaggerated belief in international agreements and the willingness of governments to adhere to them. Yet unless the more fundamental questions are addressed, it may be that castles of sand are being built. The practice of planning with children has to go hand-in-hand with a rigorous analysis of structural problems which, because their effects are far-reaching, can easily swamp the best-intentioned intervention programmes in neighbourhoods. This should not deter professionals from developing planning with children. Indeed, the dissemination of their practice can be a significant influence on governments, showing them how children's participation can be supported and thereby maintaining pressure on them to act in the interests of children.

We suspect, however, that it will be the voices and actions of children themselves which will often be the decisive factor in bringing about changes in public attitudes and government policies. As the contributions of children to this book have demonstrated, there is an abundance of energy and ideas among children. Professionals can play a key part in supporting it.

Children and young people – hopes for the future? © Ed Freeman

References

Acheson, D. (1998) *Report of the Independent Inquiry into Inequalities in Health*, London: The Stationery Office.

Adams, E. and Ingham, S. (1998) *Children's participation in environmental planning*, London: The Children's Society.

Adams, R. (1995) 'Places of childhood', in P. Henderson (ed) *Children and communities*, London: Pluto Press.

AMA (Association of Metropolitan Authorities)/CRO (Children's Rights Office), UK (1995) *Checklist for children: Local authorities and the UN Convention on the Rights of the Child*, London: AMA/CRO.

Arnstein, S. (1969) 'A ladder of citizen participation', *Journal of the American Institute of Planners*, vol 35, no 4, pp 216-24.

Association for the Protection of All Children (undated) *13,000,000 citizens with no voice in government*, London: Association for the Protection of All Children.

Atkinson, R. and Moon, G. (1994) *Urban policy in Britain: The city, the state and the market*, Basingstoke: Macmillan.

Audit Commission (1989) *Urban regeneration and economic development*, London: HMSO.

Bannerjee, T. and Lynch, K. (1977) 'On people and places: a comparative study of the spatial environment of adolescence', *Town Planning Review*, no 48, pp 105-15.

Barr, A., Hashagen, S. and Purcell, R. (1996) *Measuring community development in Northern Ireland. A handbook for practitioners*, Belfast: DHSS.

Barry, M. (1996) 'The empowering process: leading from behind', *Youth and Policy*, issue 54 (Autumn), pp 1- 12.

Boyden, J. with Holden, P. (1991) *Children of cities*, London: Zed Books.

Brookins, G.K., Petersen, A.C. and Brooks, L.M. (1997) 'Youth and families in the inner city: informing positive outcomes', in H.J. Walberg, O. Reyes and R.P. Weissberg (eds) *Children and youth: Interdisciplinary perspectives*, Chicago, IL: Sage Publications.

Callaghan, J. and Dennis, S. (1997) *Right up our street. Research with children – their account of living in East Cleveland*, London: The Children's Society.

CDF (Community Development Foundation) (1997) *Regeneration and the community: Guidelines to the community involvement aspect of the SRB Challenge Fund*, London: CDF

CDF (1998) *Briefing papers on children's participation*, London: CDF Publications.

Chanan G. (1992) *Out of the shadows*, Dublin: European Foundation for the Improvement of Living and Working Conditions.

Chanan, G. and West, A. (1999) *Regeneration and sustainable communities*, London: CDF Publications.

Children's Rights Development Unit (1994) *UK agenda for children: Environment*, London: Children's Rights Development Unit.

Children's Society, The (1997) *Children and neighbourhoods in London programme*, London: The Children's Society.

Christchurch City Council (1996) *The children's strategy study*, Christchurch, New Zealand: Christchurch City Council.

Clifton, J. and Hodgson, D. (1997) 'Rethinking practice through a children's rights perspective', in C. Cannan and C. Warren (eds) *Social action with children and families*, London: Routledge.

Community Matters (1996) *Environmental Action Pack*, London: Community Matters.

Connolly, P. (1995) 'Seen but never heard: rethinking approaches to researching racism and young children', *Discourse: Studies in the Politics of Education*, vol 17, no 2, pp 171-85.

Corsaro, W.A. (1997) *The sociology of childhood*, London: Sage Publications.

Council for Environmental Education (1995) *Environmental youth work good practice: Criteria and case studies*, Reading: Council for Environmental Education.

Craske, S. (1995) 'Chronicles of a neighbourhood park', *Streetwise*, vol 21, no 6, pp 8-11.

Cullingford, C. (1992) *Children and society: Children's attitudes to politics and power*, London: Cassell.

Geddes, M. (1997) *Partnership against poverty and exclusion?*, Bristol: The Policy Press.

Gilchrist, A. (1995) *Community development and networking*, London: CDF Publications.

Gleeson, B. (1999) *Geographies of disability*, London: Routledge.

Greenhaigh, L. and Worpole, K. (1995) 'Young people and parks', *Streetwise*, vol 21, no 1, pp 3-6.

Hart, R. (1997) *Children's participation: The theory and practice of involving young citizens in community development and environmental care*, New York, NY: UNICEF.

Hasler, J. (1995) 'Belonging and becoming: the child growing up in community', in P. Henderson (ed) *Children and communities*, London: Pluto Press.

Henderson, P. (ed.) (1988) *Working with communities*, London: The Children's Society.

Henderson, P. (ed) (1995) *Children and communities*, London: Pluto Press.

Henderson, P. (1997a) 'Community development and children: a contemporary agenda', in C. Cannan and C. Warren (eds) *Social action with children and families*, London: Routledge.

Henderson, P. (1997b) *Social inclusion and citizenship: The contribution of community development*, The Hague: Combined European Bureau for Social Development.

Henderson, P. and Mayo, M. (1998) *Training and education in urban regeneration: A framework for participants*, Bristol: The Policy Press.

Henderson, P. and Salmon, H. (1998) *Signposts to local democracy*, London: CDF Publications.

Henderson, P. and Thomas, D.N. (1987) *Skills in neighbourhood work*, London: Routledge.

Hernandez, D.J. (1993) 'The historical transformation of childhood, children's statistics and social policy', *Childhood*, vol 1, pp 187-201.

Hill, M. and Tisdall, K. (1997) *Children and society*, London: Longman.

Hillman, M. (1993) 'One false move.... A study of children's independent mobility', in M. Hillman (ed) *Children, transport and the quality of life*, London: Policy Studies Institute.

Cunningham, C., Jones, M. and Barlow, M. with children from Goonellabah and Wyrallah Road Public Schools (1996) *Town planning and children: A case study of Lismore, New South Wales*, New South Wales, Australia: University of New England.

Daniel, P. and Ivatts, J. (1998) *Children and social policy*, Basingstoke: Macmillan.

Davis, J. and Ridge, T. (1997) *Same scenery, different lifestyle*, London: The Children's Society.

De Groot, L. (1992) 'City Challenge: competing in the urban regeneration game', *Local Economy*, vol 7, pp 196-209.

DETR (Department of the Environment, Transport and the Regions) (1998) *New Deal for Communities*, London: DETR.

DoE (Department of the Environment) (1988) *Action for cities*, London: HMSO.

Dwivedi, K. N. and Varma, V.P. (eds) (1996) *Meeting the needs of ethn minority children: A handbook for professionals*, London: Jessica Kingsle

Edmonds, B.C. and Fernekes, W.R. (1996) *Children's rights: A refere handbook*, Santa Barbara, CA: ABC-CLIO Inc.

Englebert, A. (1994) 'Worlds of childhood, differentiated but differ Implications for social policy', in J. Qvortrup, M. Bardy, G.B. Sg and H. Wintersberger (eds) *Childhood matters: Social theory, practice politics*, Aldershot: Avebury, pp 285-98.

ERIC (Environment Resource and Information Centre) (1997) *Agenda 21 Case Studies*, London: ERIC, University of Westmins

Essex County Council (1998) *A design guide for residential areas*, Colc Essex County Council.

Fitzpatrick, S., Hastings, S. and Kintrea, K. (1998) *Including youn in urban regeneration: A lot to learn?* Bristol: The Policy Press.

Flekkoy, M.G. and Kaufman, N.H. (1997) *The partnership rigl child: Rights and responsibilities*, London: Jessica Kingsley.

Freeman, C. (1995) 'The changing nature of children's envir experience: the shrinking realm of outdoor play', *Internatior of Environmental Education and Information*, vol 14, no 3, pp ?

Hills, J. (1995) *Inquiry into income and wealth*, York: Joseph Rowntree Foundation.

Hodgkin, R. (1998) 'Children's voices in the corridors of power: the case for a minister for children', in D. Utting (ed) *Children's services now and in the future*, London: National Children's Bureau.

Hodgkin, R. and Newell, P. (1996) *Effective government structures for children*, London: Calouste Gulbenkian Foundation.

Holman, B. (1997) *FARE Dealing*, London: CDF Publications.

Home Office (1998) *Supporting families: A consultation document*, London: The Stationery Office.

Hulyer, B. (1997) 'Long-term development: neighbourhood community development work on estates', in C. Cannan and C. Warren (eds) *Social action with children and families*, London: Routledge.

ISCA (International Save the Children Alliance) (undated) *A girl's right to development, equality and peace*, Geneva: ISCA.

James, A. and Prout, A. (eds) (1990) *Constructing and reconstructing childhood*, Basingstoke: Falmer.

Jenks, C. (1996) *Childhood*, London: Routledge.

Kent, G. (1995) *Children in the international political economy*, London: Macmillan.

Lansdown, G. (1995a) 'The Children's Rights Development Unit', in B. Franklin (ed) *The handbook of children's rights: Comparative policy and practice*, London: Routledge.

Lansdown, G. (1995b) *Taking part: Children's participation in decision making*, London: Institute for Public Policy Research.

Lavalette, M. (1994) *Child employment in the capitalist labour market*, Aldershot: Avebury.

Leeds City Council (1996) *Leeds listens ... to children and young people*, Leeds: Leeds City Council.

Lennard, H.L. and Crowhurst-Lennard, S.H. (1992) 'Children in public places: some lessons from European cities', *Children's Environments*, vol 9, no 2, pp 37-47.

Lestor, J. (1996) 'A minister for children', in B. Franklin (ed) *The handbook of children's rights: Comparative policy and practice*, London: Routledge.

Liverpool 8 Children's Research Group (1997) *Listen to the children*, Liverpool: Liverpool 8 Children's Group.

McKay, D. and Cox, A. (1979) *The politics of urban change*, London: Croom Helm.

Matthews, H. and Limb, M. (1998) 'The right to say. The development of youth councils/forums in the UK', *Area*, vol 30, no 1, pp 66-78.

Matthews, H. and Limb, M. (1999) 'Defining an agenda for the geography of children: review and prospect', *Progress in Human Geography*, vol 23, no 1, pp 61-90.

May, N. (1997) *Challenging assumptions: Gender issues in urban regeneration*, York: Joseph Rowntree Foundation.

Mental Health Foundation (1999) *Bright futures*, London: Mental Health Foundation.

Millward, A. and Wheway, R. (1997) 'Facilitating play on housing estates', in *Findings*, no 217, York: Joseph Rowntree Foundation.

Morrow, V. (1994) 'Responsible children? Aspects of children's work and employment outside school in contemporary UK', in B. Mayall (ed) *Children's childhood: Observed and experienced*, London: Falmer.

Moss, P. and Petrie, P. (1997) *Children's services: Time for a new approach*, London: Institute of Education, University of London.

National Voluntary Council for Children's Play (1994) *A Charter for Children's Play*, London: National Children's Bureau.

Newell, P. (1995) 'Rights, participation and neighbourhoods', in P. Henderson (ed) *Children and communities*, London: Pluto Press.

Nieuwenhuys, O. (1997) 'Spaces for the children of the urban poor: experiences with participatory action research (PAR)', *Environment and Urbanisation*, vol 9, no 1, pp 233-48.

Owen, S. (1991) *Planning settlements naturally*, Chichester: Packard Publishing.

Peace Child International (1994) *Rescue mission Planet Earth: A children's edition of Local Agenda 21*, London: Kingfisher Books.

Pettitt, B. (ed) (1998) *Children and work in the UK*, London: Child Poverty Action Group.

Postman, N. (1994) *The disappearance of childhood*, New York, NY: Vintage Books.

Prout, A. and James, A. (1990) 'A new paradigm for the sociology of childhood? Provenance, promise and problems', in A. James and A. Prout (eds) (1990) *Constructing and reconstructing childhood*, Basingstoke: Falmer.

Pugh, G. and Rouse-Selleck, D. (1996) 'Listening to and communicating with young children', in R. Davie, G. Upton and V. Varma (eds) *The voice of the child: A handbook for professionals*, London: Falmer.

Q2000 (1995) 'The Swedish implementation of Local Agenda 21 and the role of Q2000 Youth Campaign for a Sustainable Sweden', *Local Government Policy Making*, vol 22, no 2, pp 77-81.

Qvortrup, J. (1991) *Childhood as a social phenomenon – An introduction to a series of national reports*, Vienna: European Centre for Social Welfare Policy and Research.

Qvortrup, J. (1994) 'A new solidarity contract? The significance of a demographic balance for the welfare of children and the elderly', in J. Qvortrup, M. Bardy, G.B. Sgritta and H. Wintersberger (eds) *Childhood matters: Social theory, practice and politics*, Aldershot: Avebury, pp 319-34.

Roche, J. and Tucker, S. (1997) 'Youth in society: contemporary theory, policy and practice', in J. Roche and S. Tucker (eds) *Youth in society*, London: Sage Publications.

Rosenbaum, M. (1993) *Children and the environment*, London: National Children's Bureau.

Ross, E. (1996) 'Learning to listen to children', in R. Davie, G. Upton and V. Varma (eds) *The voice of the child: A handbook for professionals*, London: Falmer.

Ruse, S. (1997) *Children, young people and the environment*, Leeds: Leeds Environment City Initiative.

Saporiti, A. (1994) 'A methodology for making children count', in J. Qvortrup, M. Bardy, G.B. Sgritta and H. Wintersberger (eds) *Childhood matters: Social theory, practice and politics*, Aldershot: Avebury, pp 189-210.

Save the Children (1997) *All together now: Community participation for children and young people*, London: Save the Children.

Schoenberg, S. (1979) 'Criteria for the evaluation of neighbourhood viability in working class and low income areas in core cities', *Social Problems*, vol 27, no 1, pp 69-78.

Sgritta, G.B. (1994) 'The generational division of welfare', in J. Qvortrup, M. Bardy, G.B. Sgritta and H Wintersberger (eds) *Childhood matters: Social theory, practice and politics*, Aldershot: Avebury, pp 335-61.

Sills, A.F., Taylor, G. and Golding, P. (1988) *The politics of the urban crisis*, London: Hutchison.

Skelcher, C., McCabe, A., Lowndes, V. with Nanton, P. (1996) *Community networks in regeneration: It all depends on who you know...!*, Bristol: The Policy Press.

Smith, M.K. (1994) *Local education*, Buckingham: Open University Press.

Smith, T. (1993) *Family centres and bringing up young children*, London: The Children's Society and DoH.

Social Exclusion Unit (1998) *Bringing Britain together: A national strategy for neighbourhood renewal*, London: Cabinet Office.

Sparks, I. (1995) 'The shape of childhood in 2001', *Children and Society*, vol 9, no 3, pp 5-16.

Stewart, M. and Taylor, M. (1995) *Empowerment and estate regeneration: A critical review*, Bristol: The Policy Press.

Talbot, J. (1988) 'Have enterprise zones encouraged enterprise?', *Regional Studies*, vol 22, pp 507-14.

Taylor, M. (1995) *Unleashing the potential: Bringing residents to the centre of regeneration*, York: Joseph Rowntree Foundation.

Thake, S. (1995) *Staying the course: The role and structures of community regeneration organisations*, York: Joseph Rowntree Foundation.

Tranter, P. (1993) *Children's mobility in Canberra, Australia*, Canberra, Australia: University of New South Wales.

UNICEF (1995) *The Convention on the Rights of the Child*, London: UK Committee for UNICEF.

Wadhams, C. (1998) *Thursday's children*, Bath: The Quest Trust.

Ward, C. (1978) *The child in the city*, London: Architectural Press.

Walker, R. (ed) (1999) *Ending child poverty: Popular welfare for the 21st century?*, Bristol: The Policy Press.

West, A, (1998) 'What about the children? The involvement of younger residents', in C. Cooper and M. Hawtin (eds) *Resident involvement and community action: From theory to practice*, Coventry: Chartered Institute of Housing.

Willow, C. (1997) *Hear! Hear! Promoting children and young people's democratic participation in local government*, London: Local Government Information Unit.

Wood, A. (1999) *Looking down the other end of the telescope: The Child Poverty Project, Glasgow*, Glasgow: Barnardo's/Stepping Stones in Scotland.

Wood, B. (1998) 'Children's consultation', in CDF, *Involving children in neighbourhoods*, Briefing Paper 4, London: CDF Publications.

World Commission on Environment and Development (1987) *Our common future*, Oxford: Oxford University Press.

Wyn, J. and White, R. (1997) *Rethinking youth*, St Leonards, Australia: Allen and Unwin.

Index

Other related titles from The Policy Press include:

Ending child poverty: Popular welfare for the 21st century?
Edited by Robert Walker
pbk 1 86134 199 7 £15.99 (1999)

Home Sweet Home? The impact of poor housing on health
Alex Marsh, David Gordon, Christina Pantazis and Pauline Heslop
pbk 1 86134 176 8 £16.99 (1999)

New poverty series edited by David Gordon
Studies in poverty, inequality and social exclusion

Inequalities in health: The evidence presented to the Independent Inquiry into Inequalities in Health, chaired by Sir Donald Acheson
Edited by David Gordon, Mary Shaw, Daniel Dorling and George Davey Smith
pbk ISBN 1 86134 174 1 £18.99 (1999)

The widening gap: Health inequalities and policy in Britain
Edited by David Gordon, Mary Shaw, Daniel Dorling and George Davey Smith
pbk ISBN 1 86134 142 3 £16.99 (1999)

Tackling inequalities: Where are we now and what can be done?
Edited by Christina Pantazis and David Gordon
pbk ISBN 1 86134 146 6 £15.99 TBC (2000)

All the above titles are available from
Biblios Publishers' Distribution Services Ltd
Star Road, Partridge Green, West Sussex RH13 8LD
Tel +44 (0)1403 710851, Fax +44 (0)1403 711143